USE AS CALENDAR COVER-UPS

Choose one pattern for monthly cover-ups on calendar dates. Duplicate the pattern on regular white paper, construction paper or lightweight tagboard. If possible, laminate these calendar cover-up patterns so they can be used again.

USE AS NAME TAGS

Choose one pattern to use as name tags for special events. Follow the same steps used to make calendar cover-ups. Print the names on the completed tags.

USE AS BULLETIN BOARD THEMES

Choose a pattern to use as a bulletin board theme. Enlarge the pattern by use of an overhead projector and the following steps:

1. Using an overhead pen, trace the pattern on a clear sheet of acetate, a plastic bag or wax paper.
2. Tape a sheet of paper or tagboard on the wall.·
3. Place the acetate sheet on the overhead projector and project the picture onto the paper or tagboard.
4. Move the overhead projector forward to make the picture smaller or move it back to enlarge the picture.
5. Trace around the projected image.

Once the enlarged image has been traced, use crayons, water pastels, colored chalk or markers to complete the sketch. Cut out the finished bulletin board picture and attach it to the desired bulletin board area. The finished picture can be used above a calendar or as part of a theme used to motivate students. Trace a related pattern for each student in the classroom, or allow students to trace their own. Label these patterns with the students' names. Inform the students of the goal they must reach (example: a perfect score on a spelling test). Once the students achieve this set goal, they may display their related patterns on the bulletin board.

USE AS STORY STARTERS

Choose a pattern for a story starter. Enlarge the pattern using the overhead projector. Print a related word list on the enlarged pattern. Students may use the story starter to create their own stories.

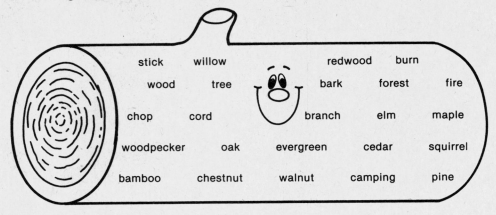

stick	willow		redwood	burn
wood	tree		bark	forest	fire
chop	cord		branch	elm	maple
woodpecker	oak	evergreen	cedar	squirrel
bamboo	chestnut	walnut	camping	pine

USE AS RACE GAMES

Choose one pattern to use as the start position of the game. Choose another pattern to use as the finish position of the game. Use the third pattern to make a path for the game. Arrange the patterns into a game format. (See example below.)

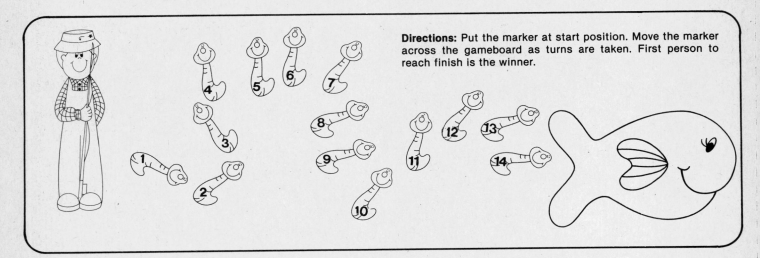

Directions: Put the marker at start position. Move the marker across the gameboard as turns are taken. First person to reach finish is the winner.

Variations for Race Gameboards:

1. Attach the gameboard to a bulletin board. Change the board for different holidays.
2. Design the game on tagboard for small groups or on file folders for partners.
3. Make a transparency of the gameboard and project it onto the chalkboard to play with the entire class or in small groups.
4. Paint the gameboard on the floor of your classroom with white shoe polish.

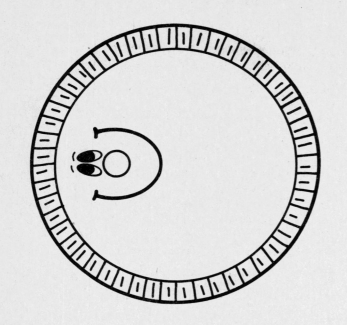

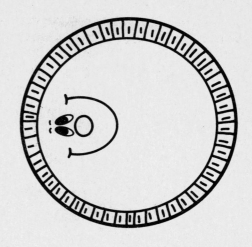

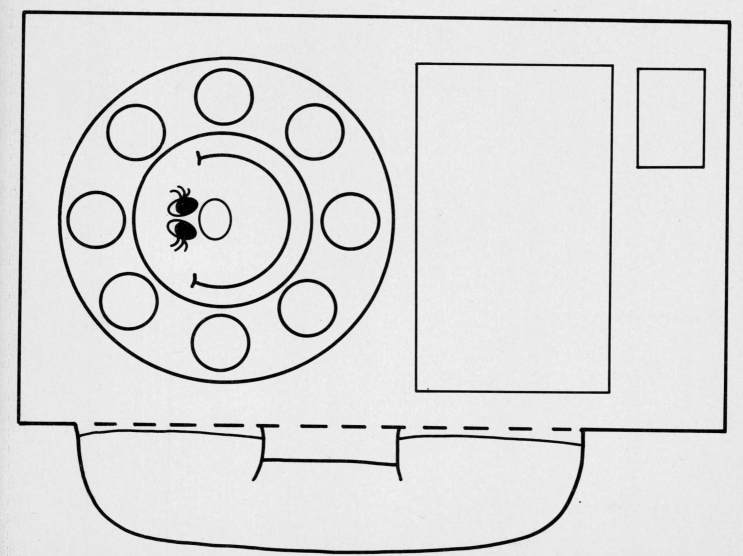

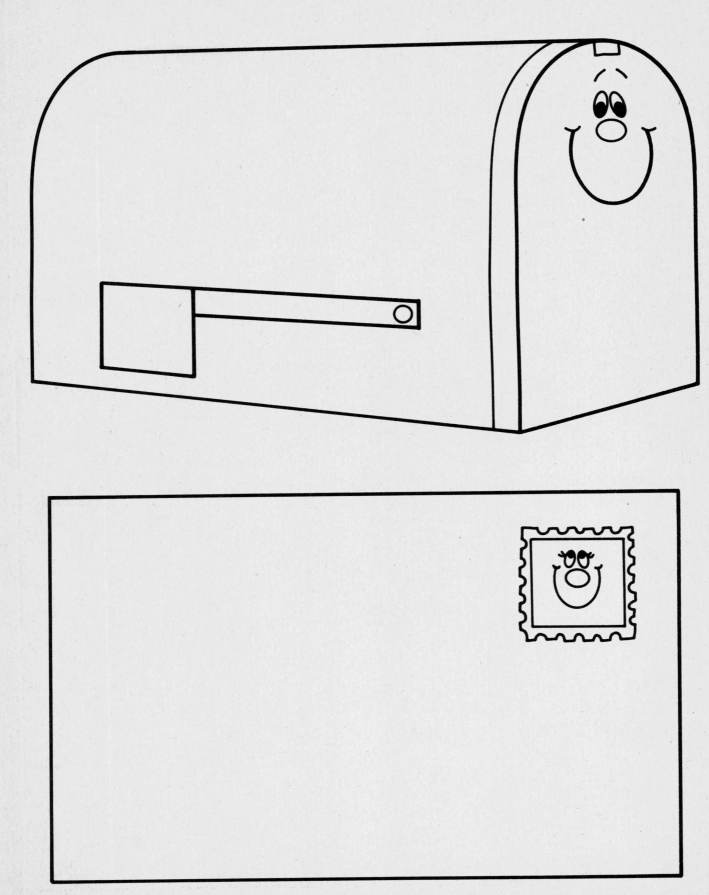

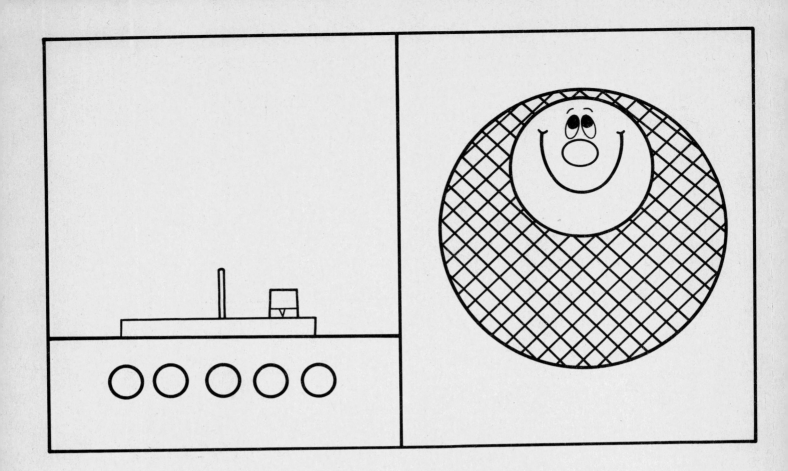

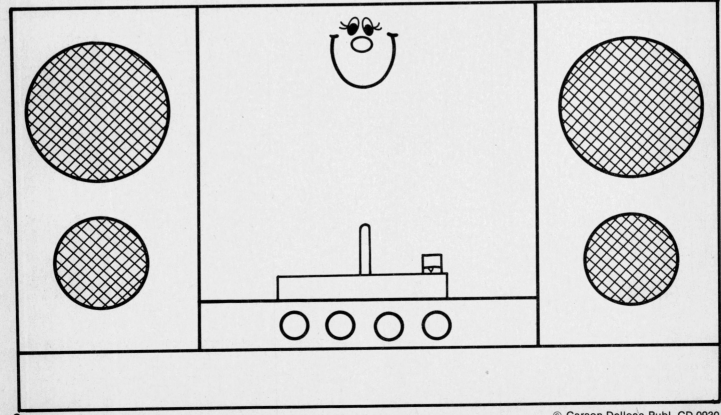

6

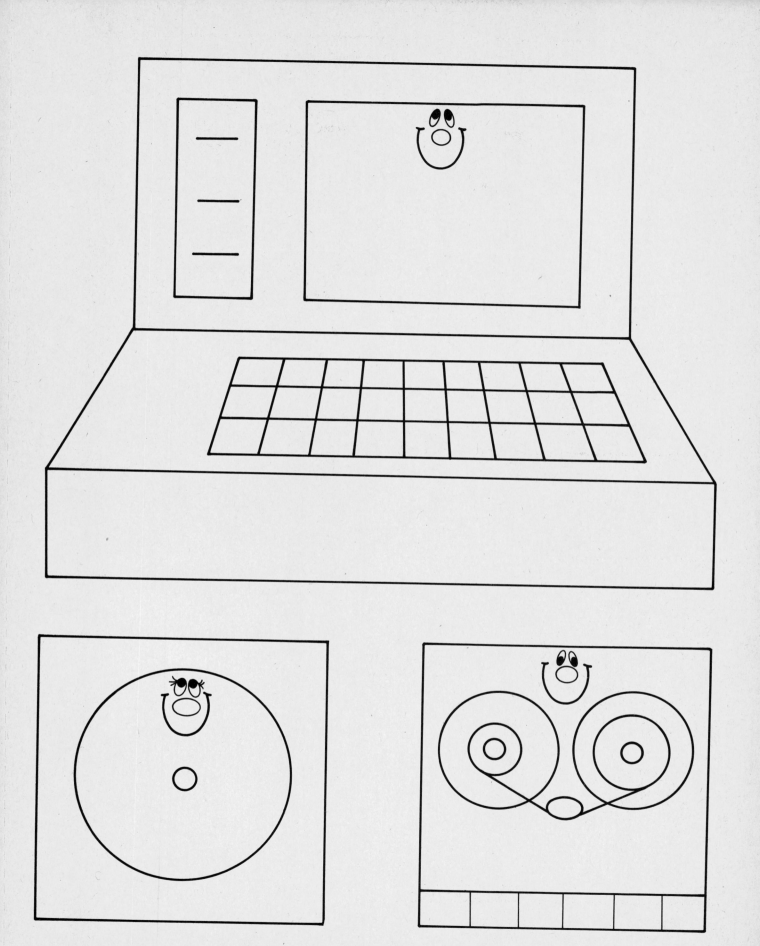

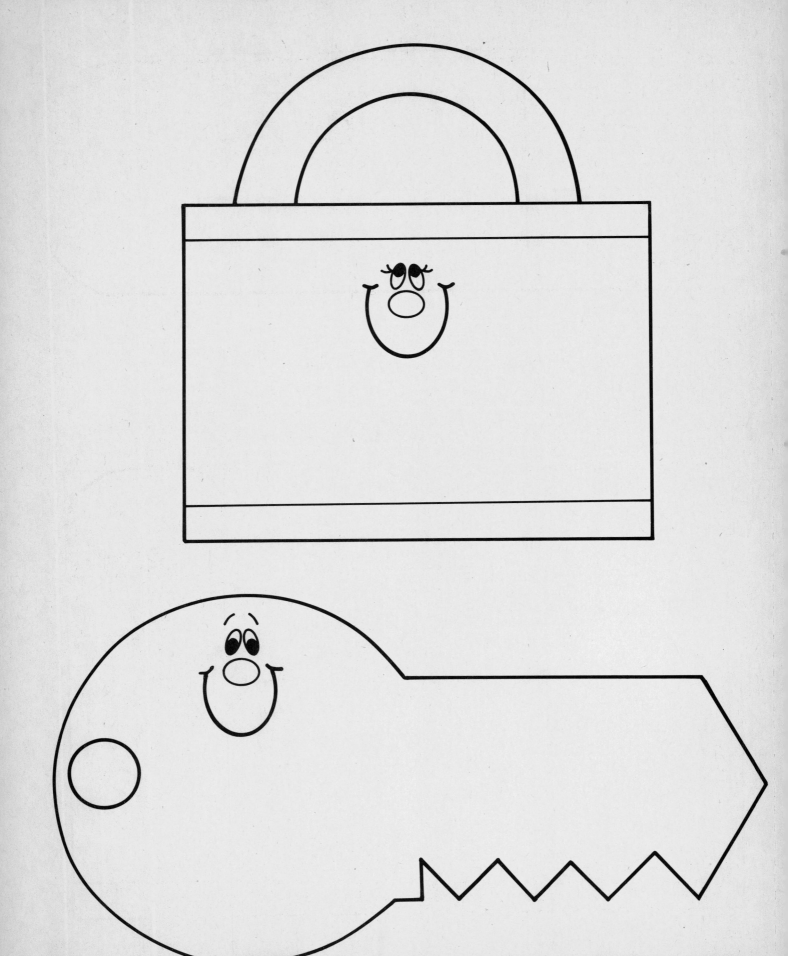

8

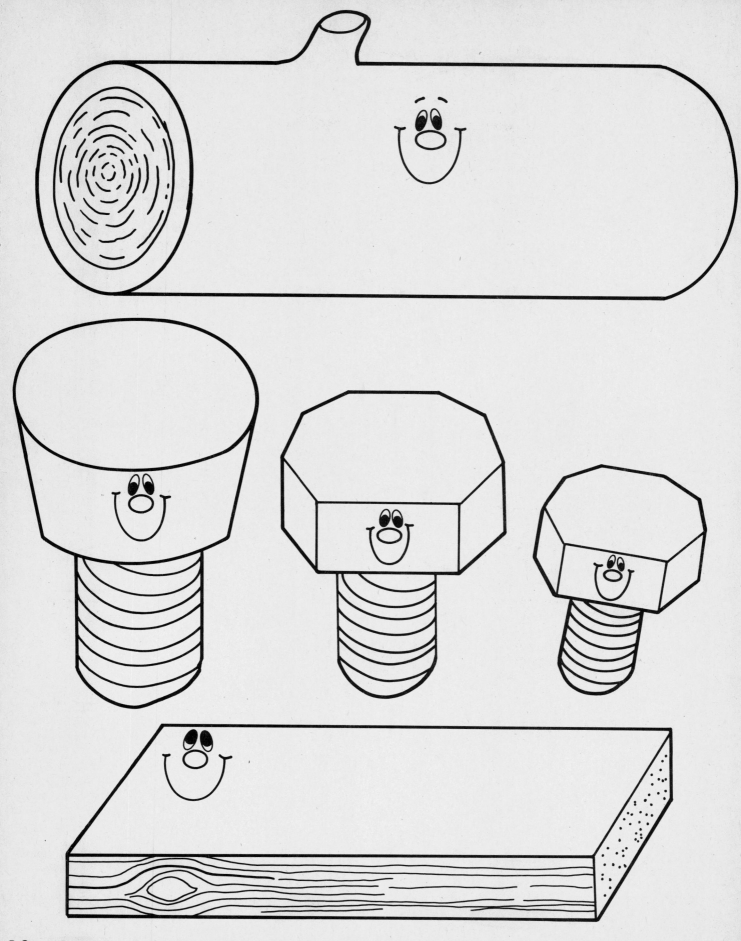

9

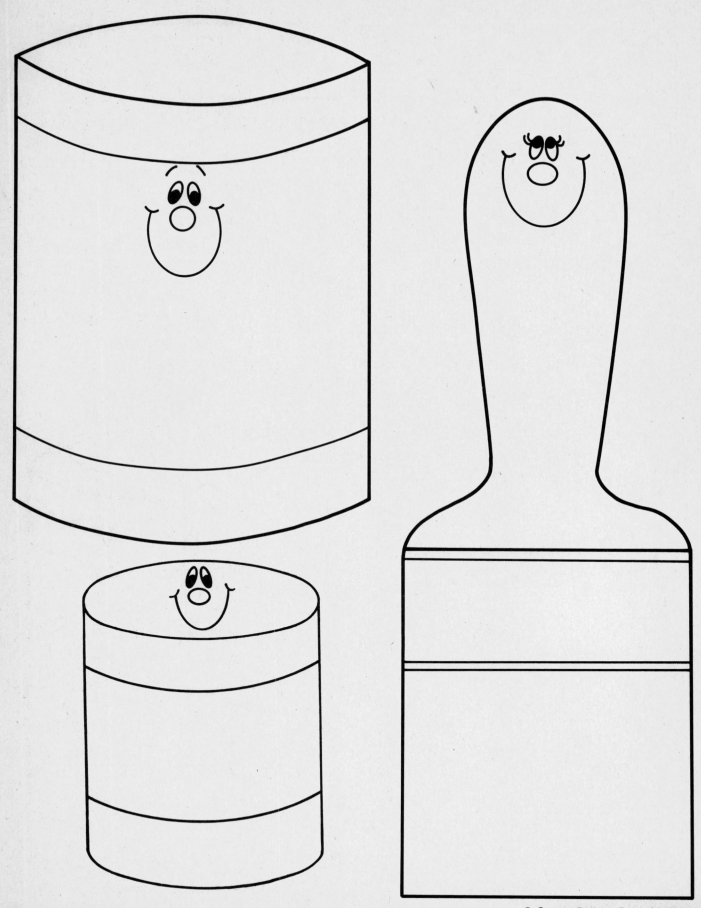

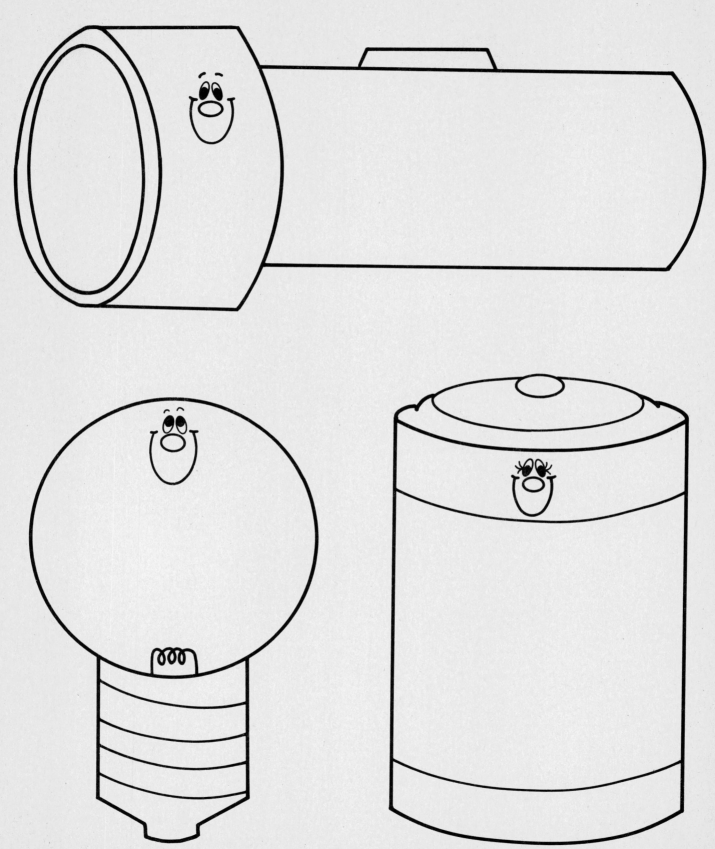

11

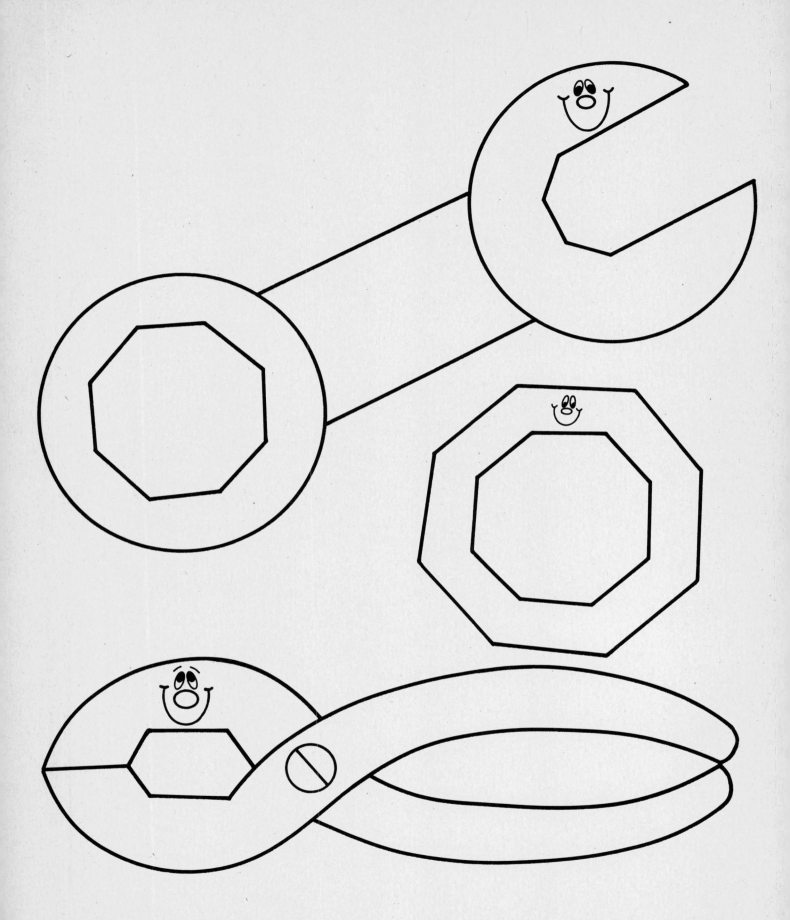

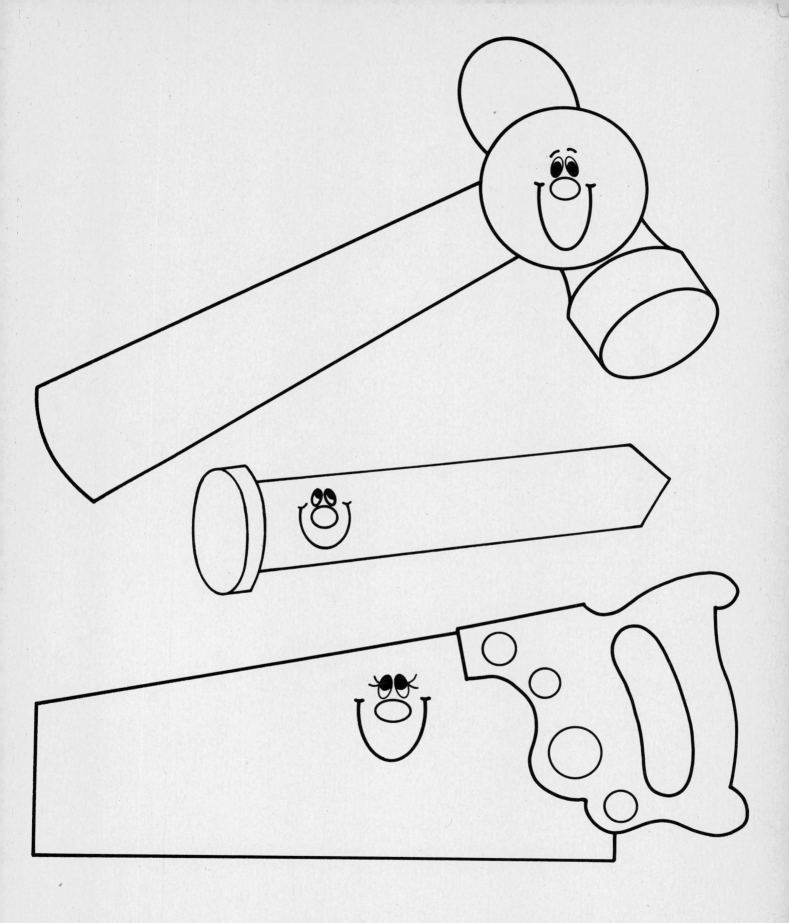

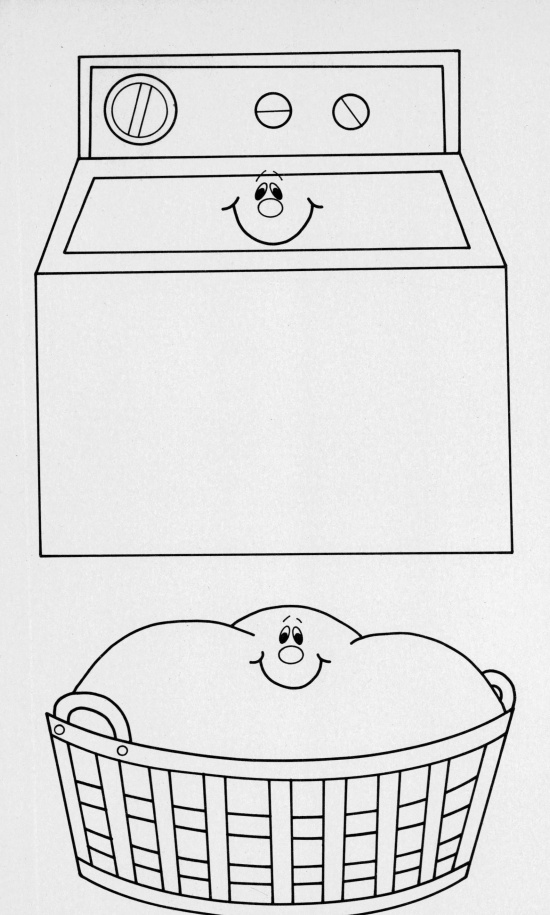

14

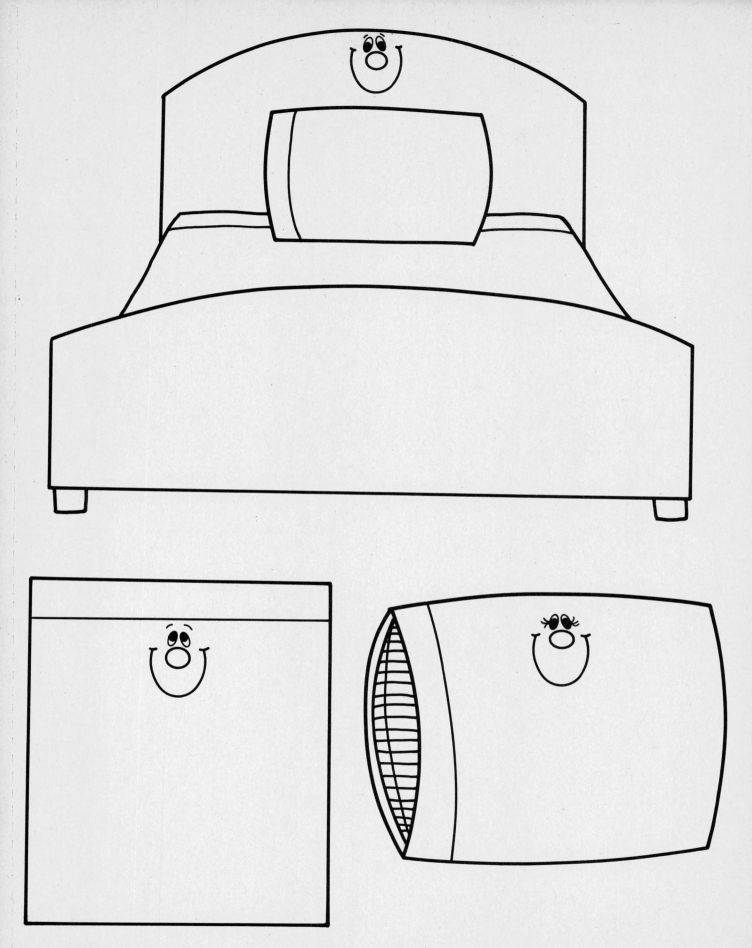

15

16

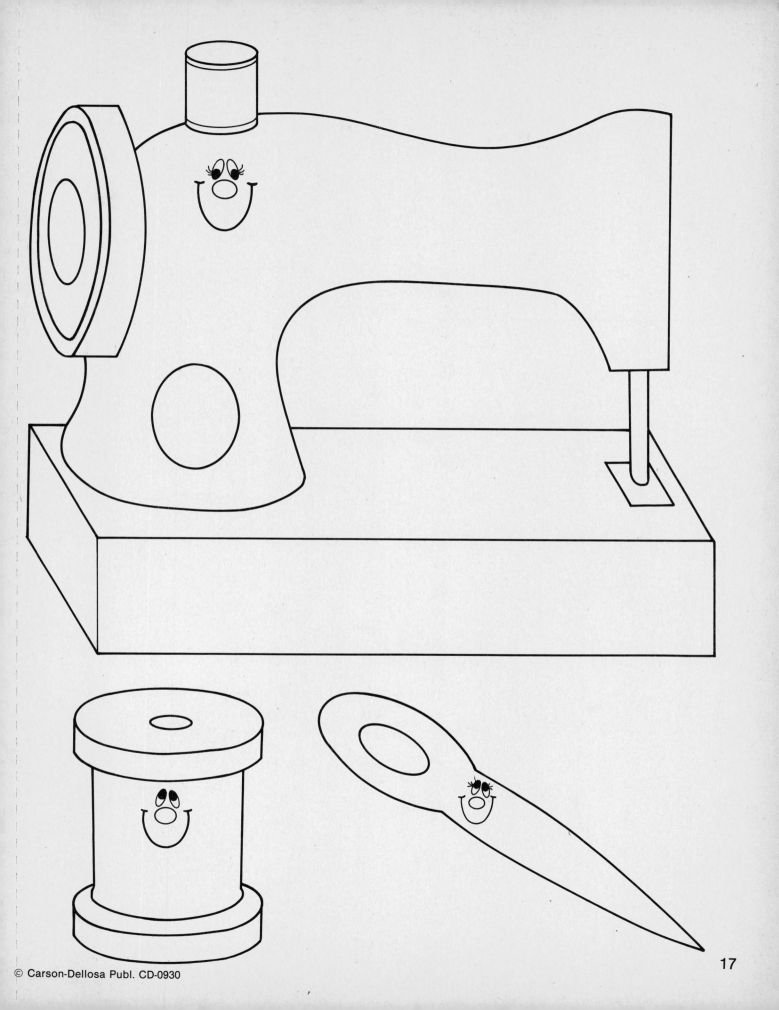

17

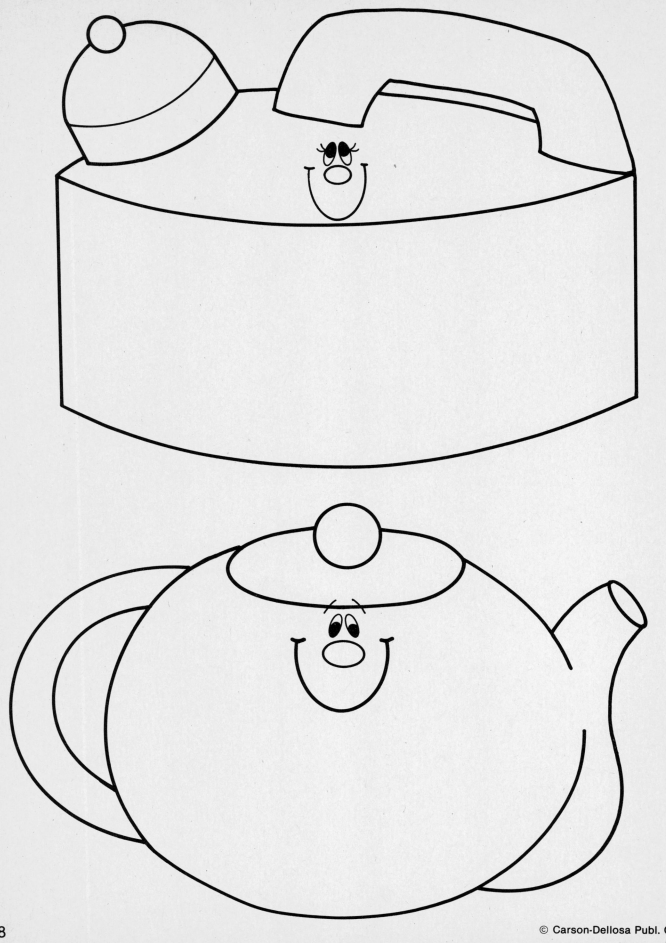

18

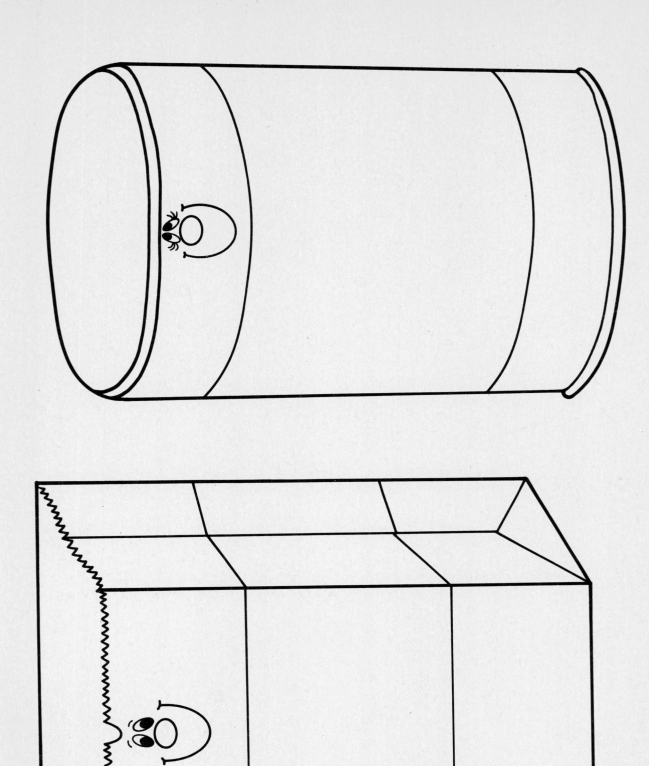

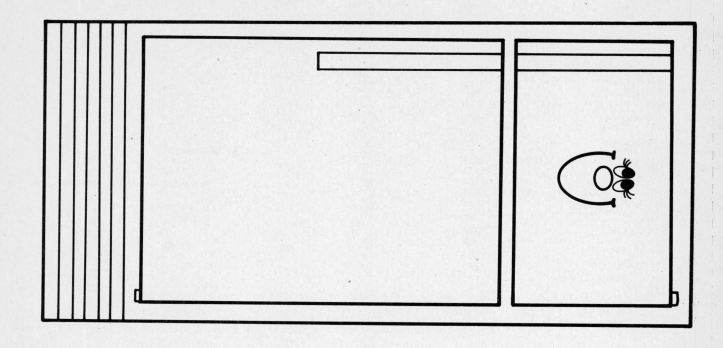

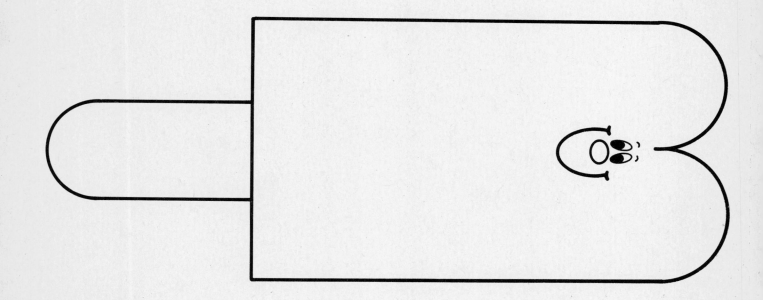

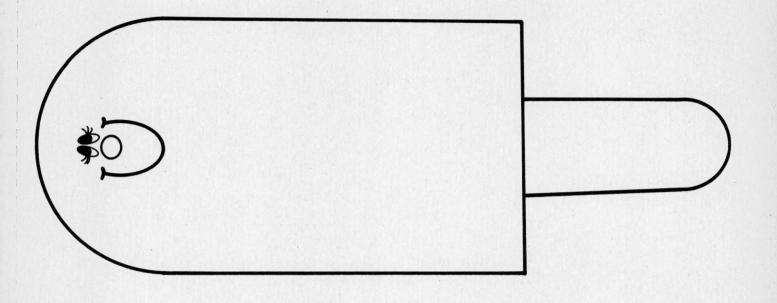

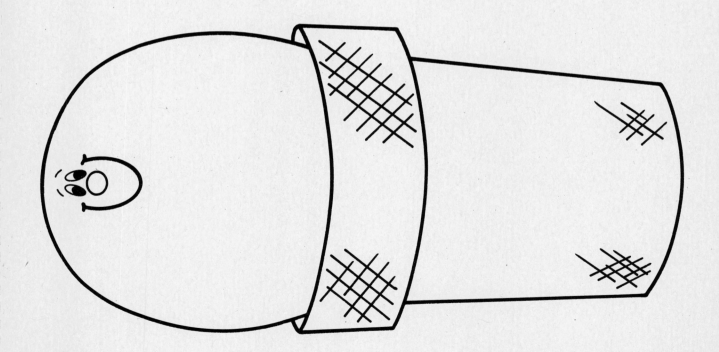

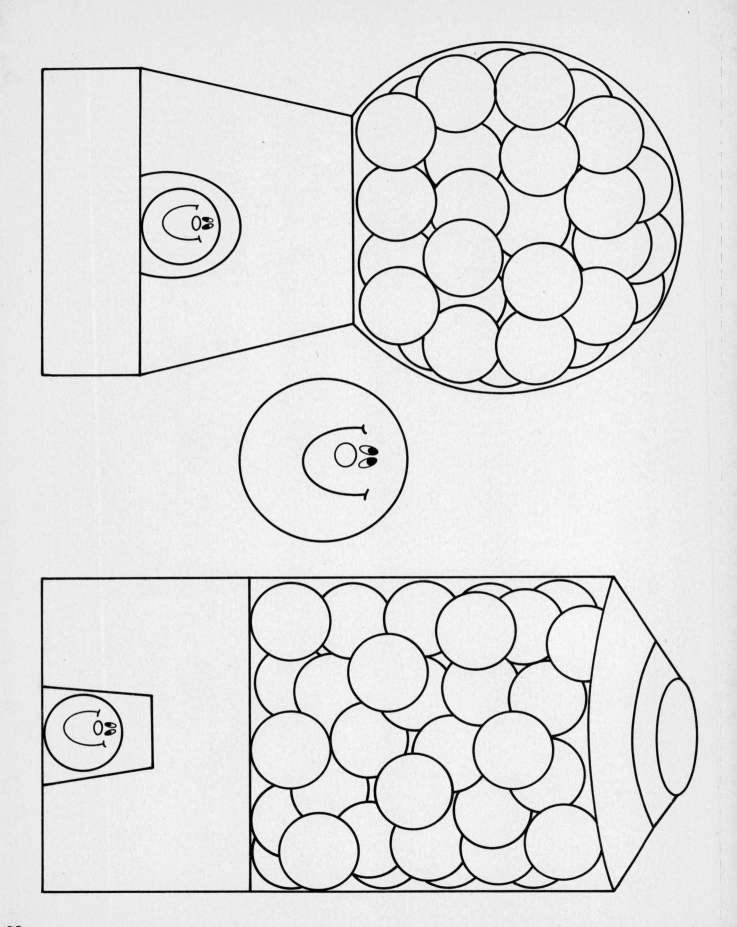

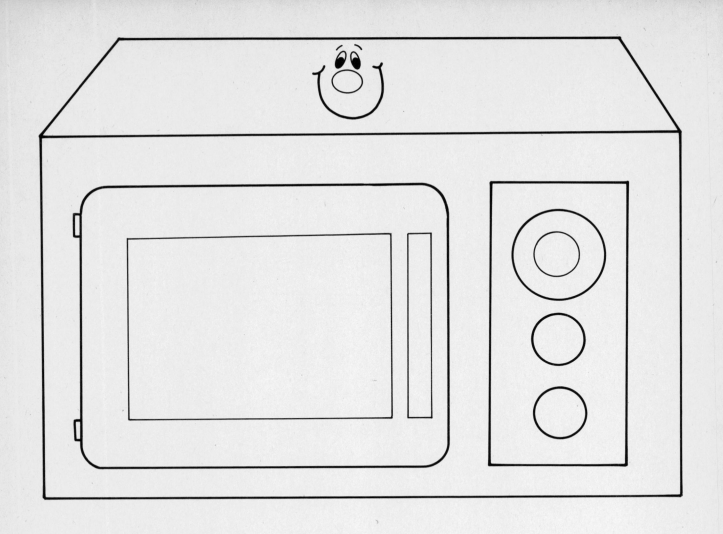

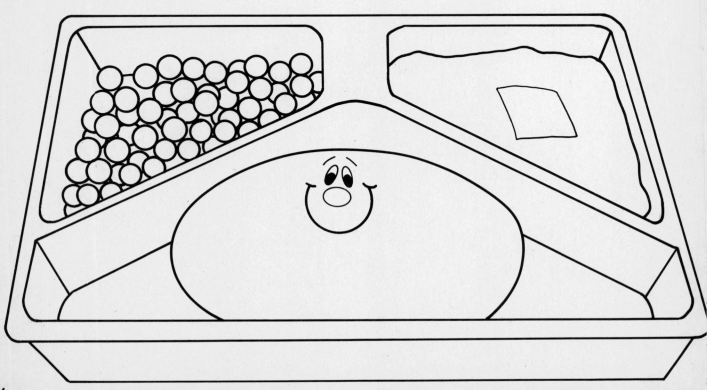

24

26

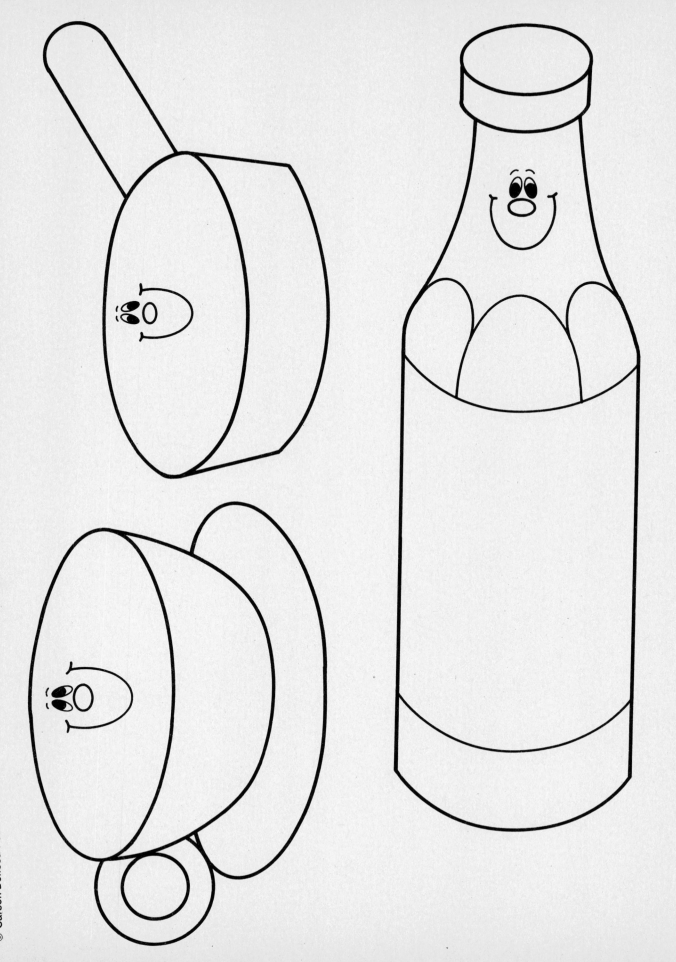

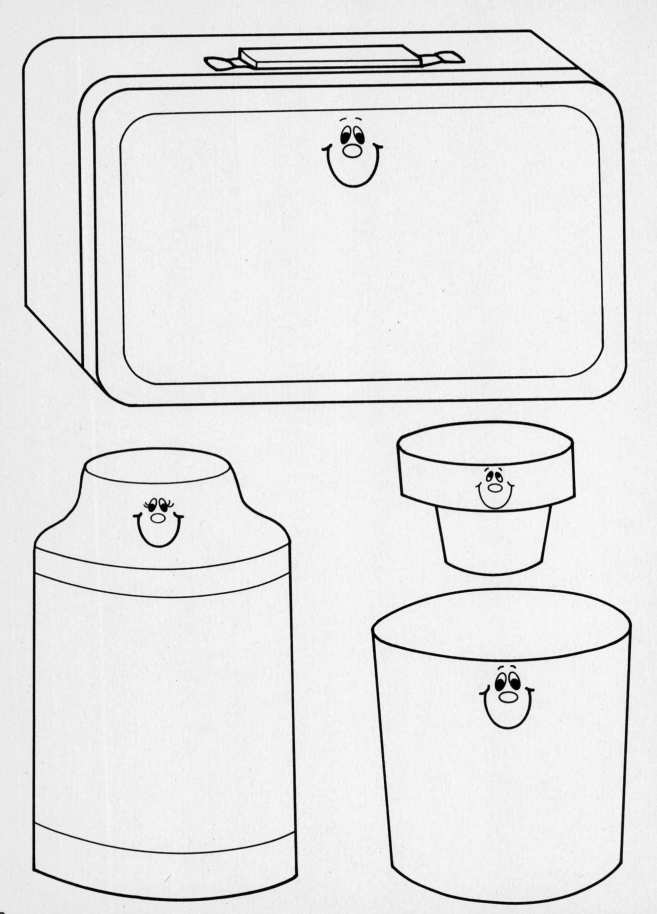

28

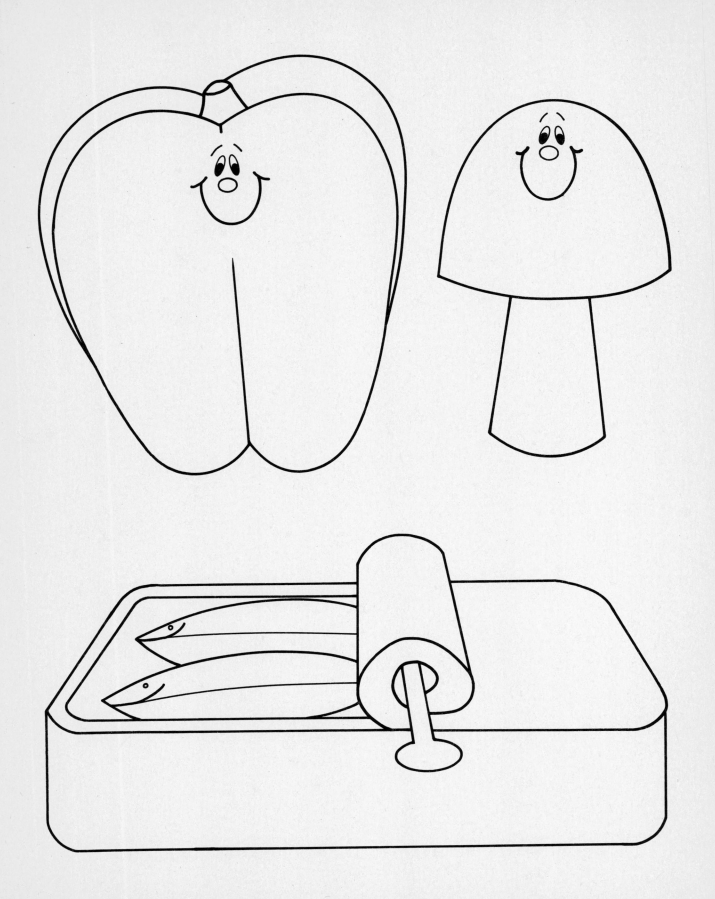

30

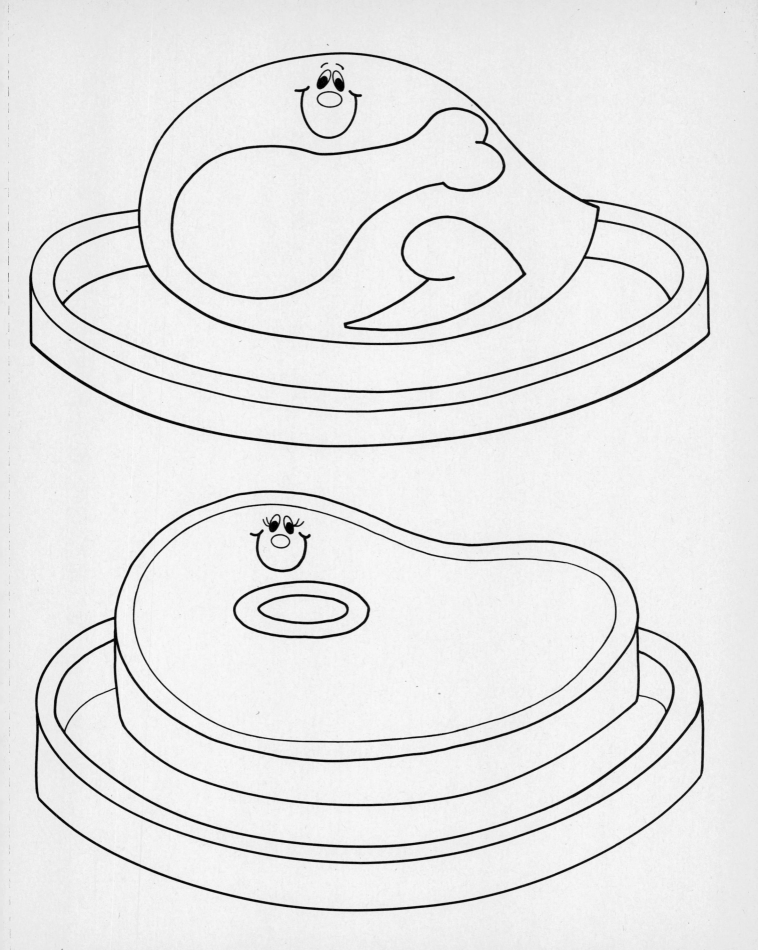

31

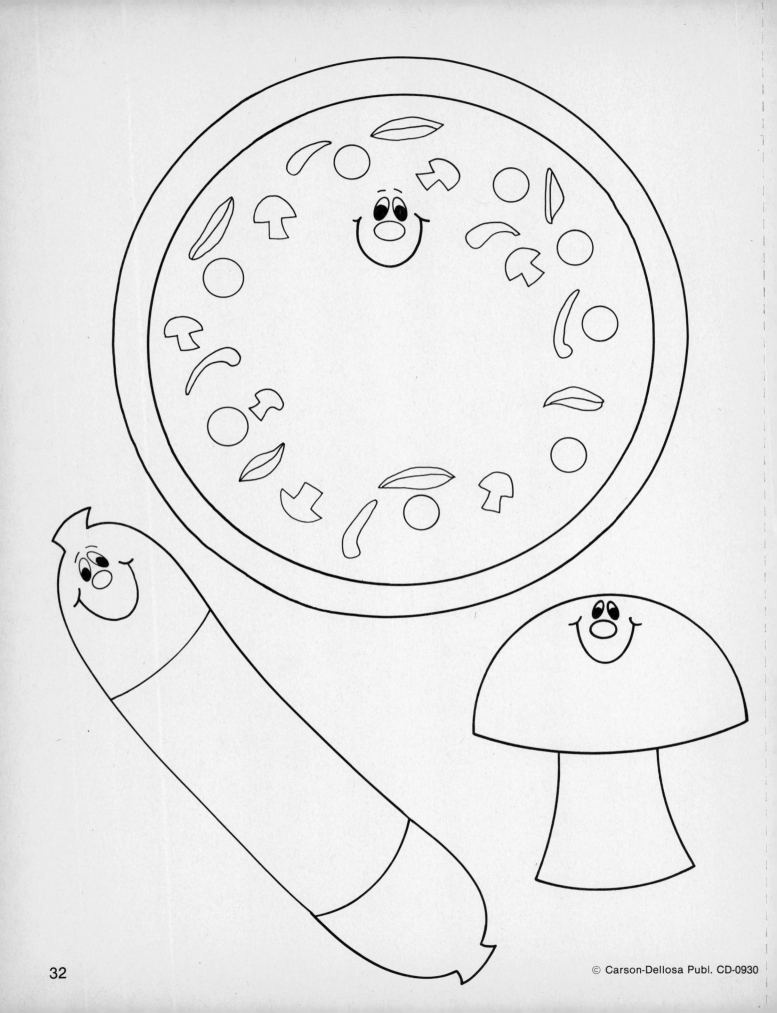

32

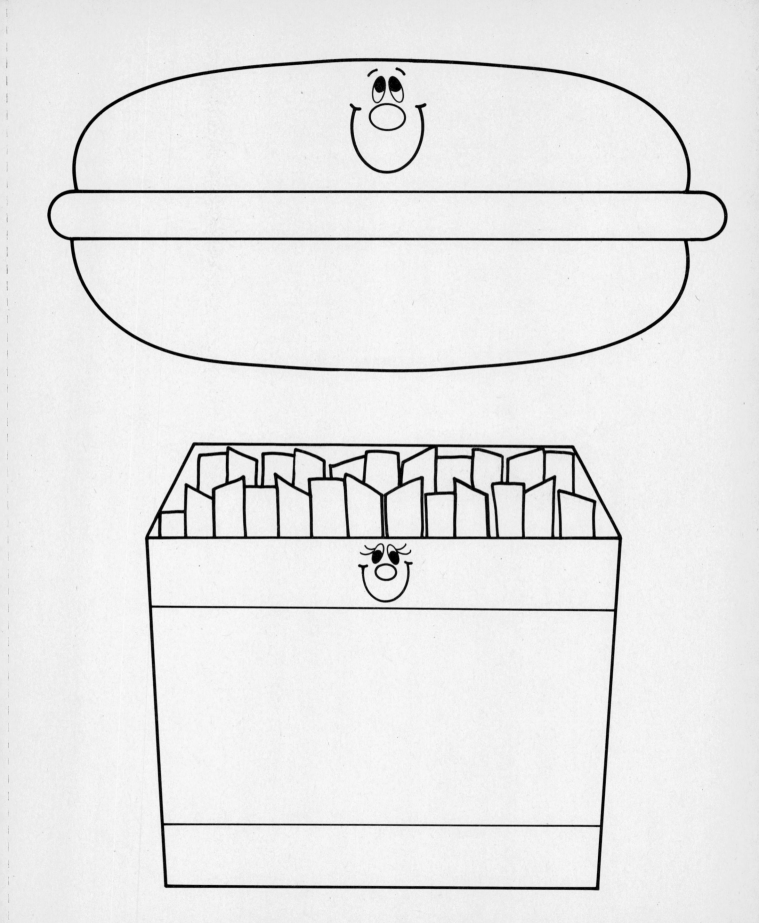

33

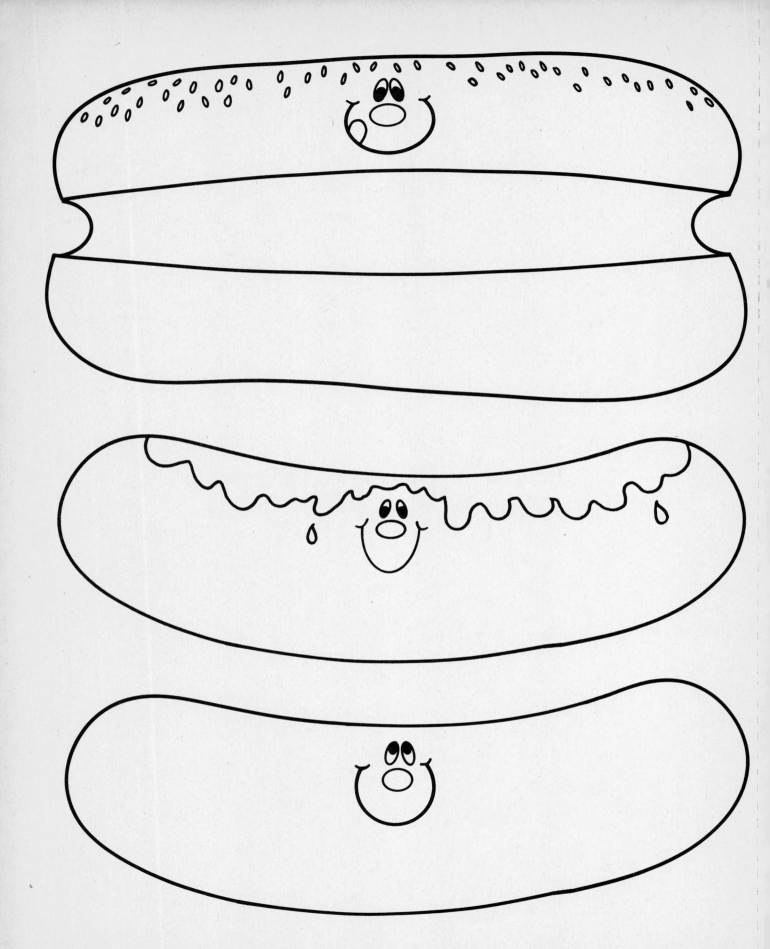

36

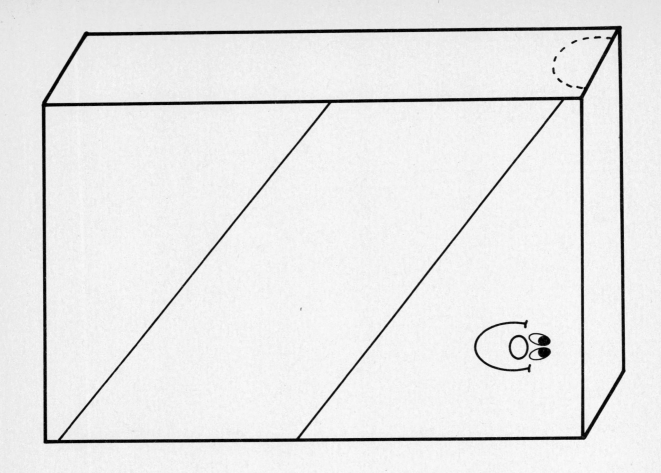

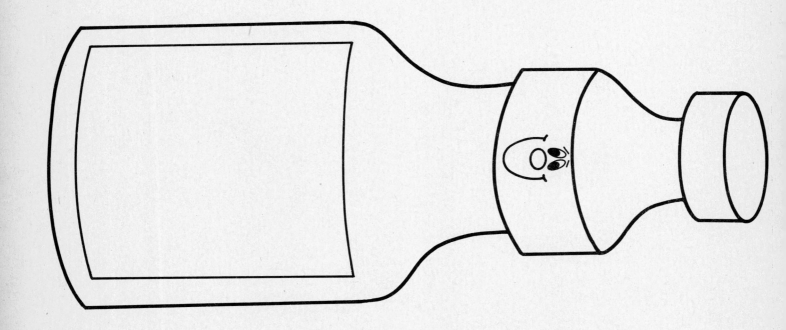

38

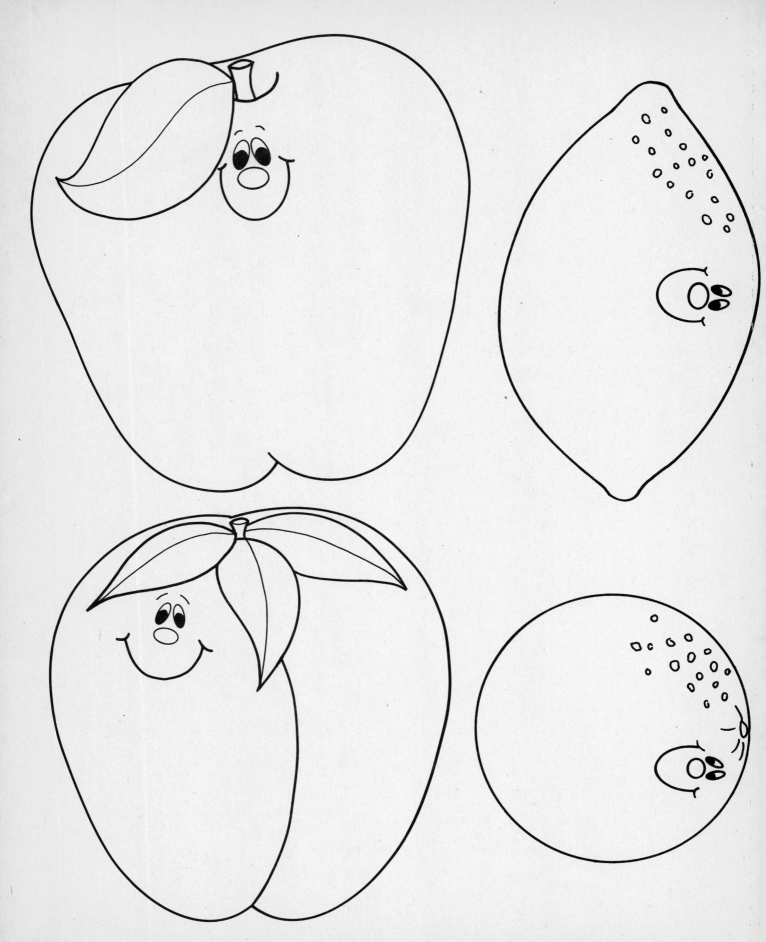

40

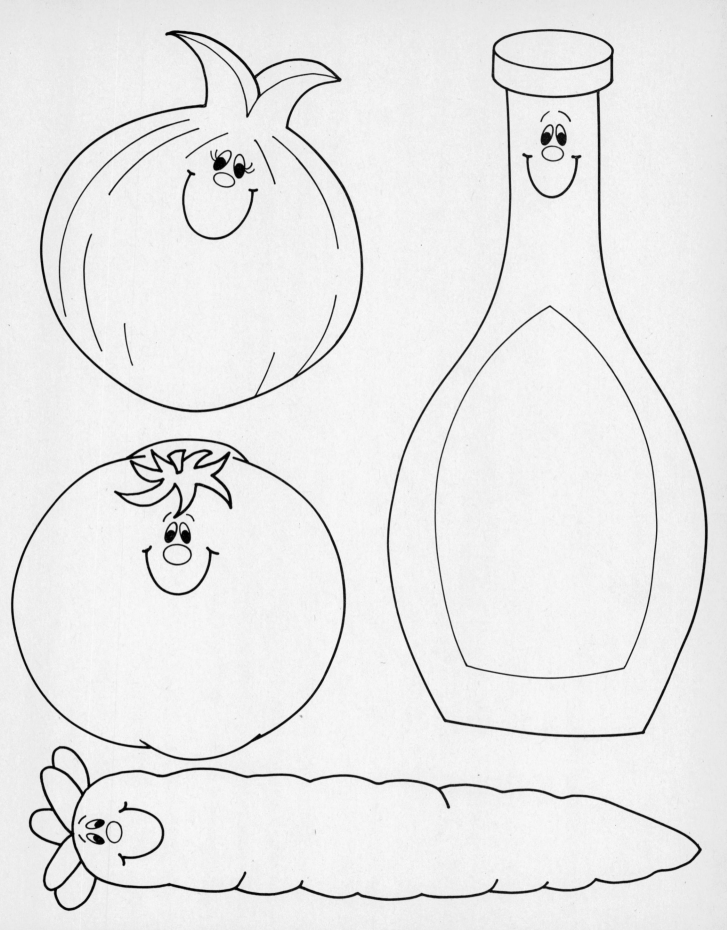

44

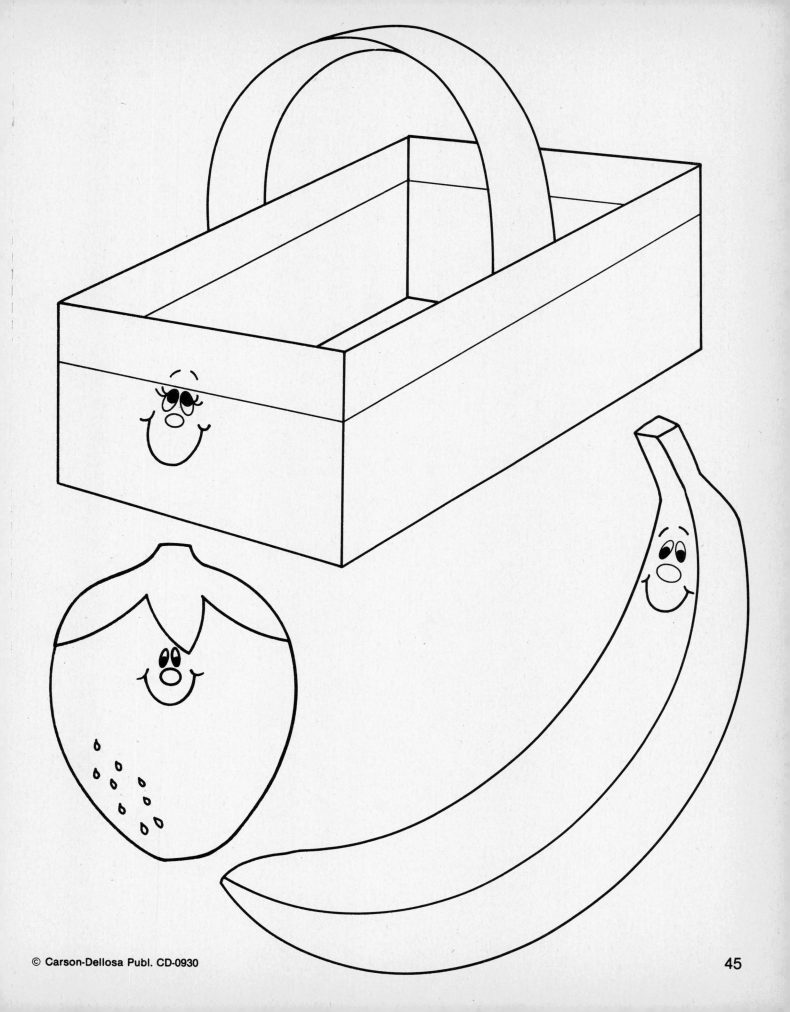

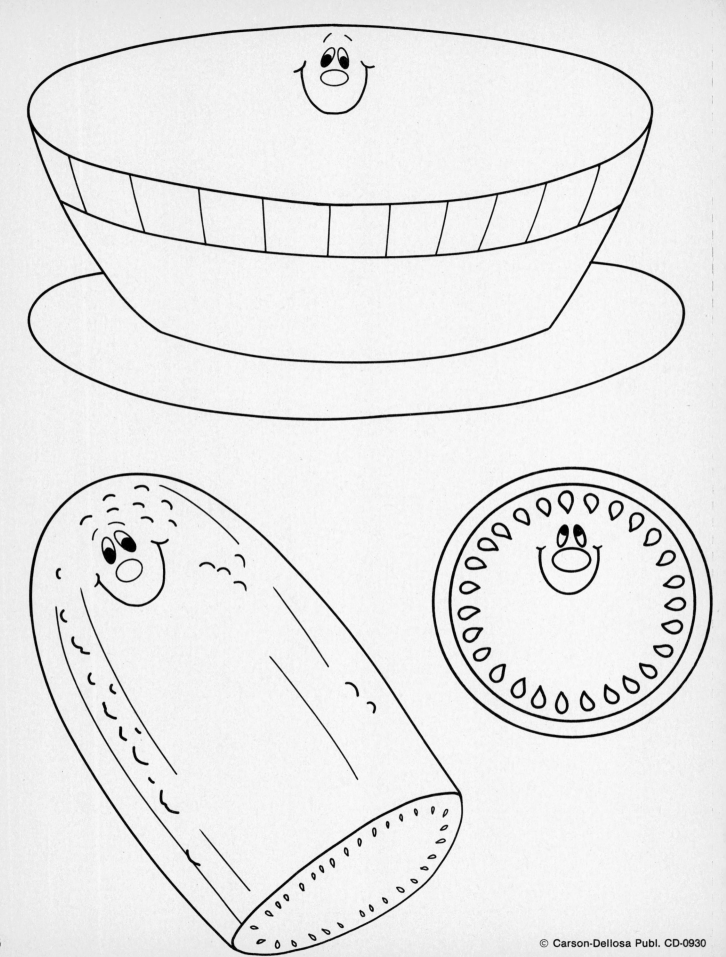

48

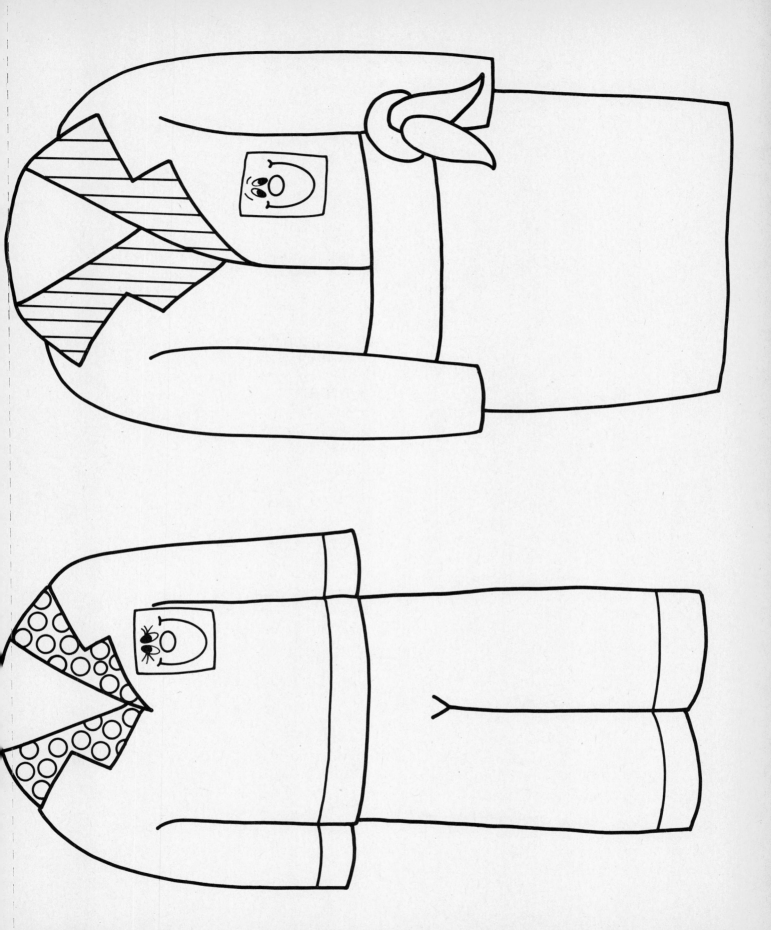

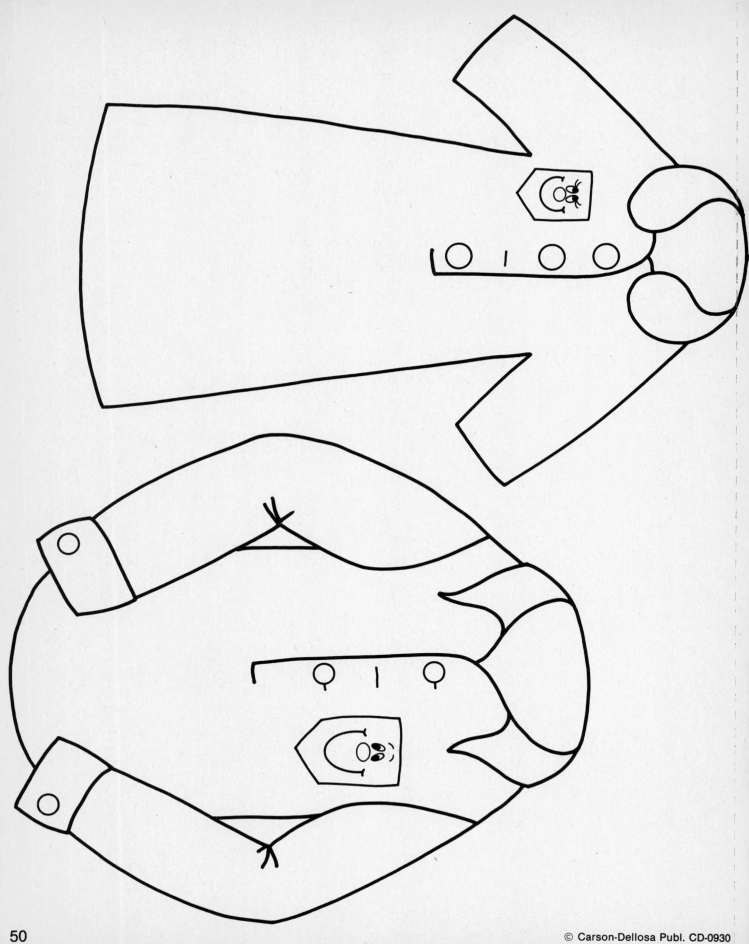

50

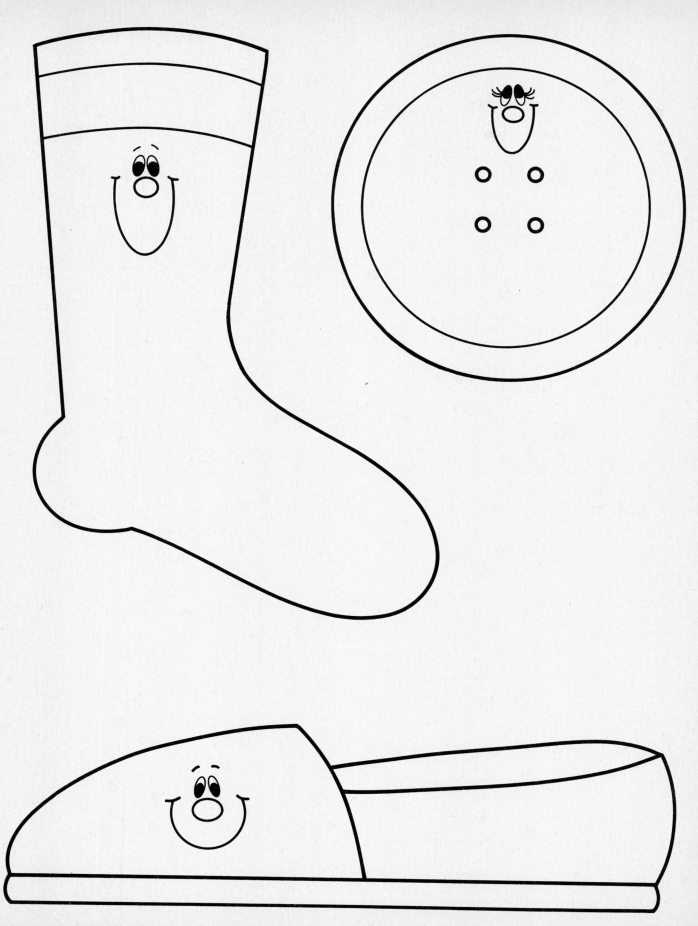

52

53

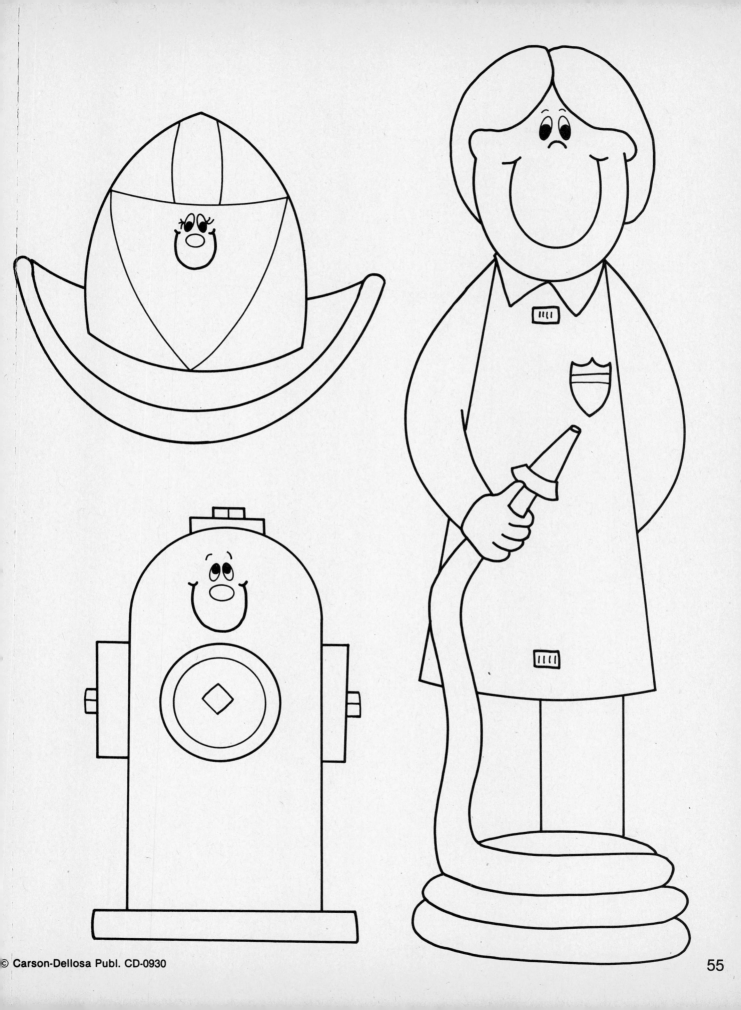

55

56

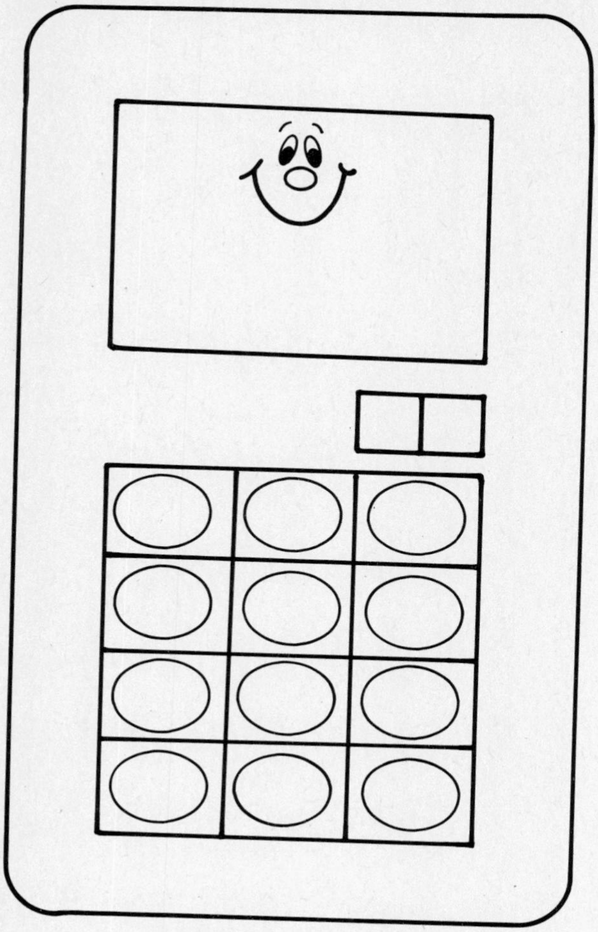

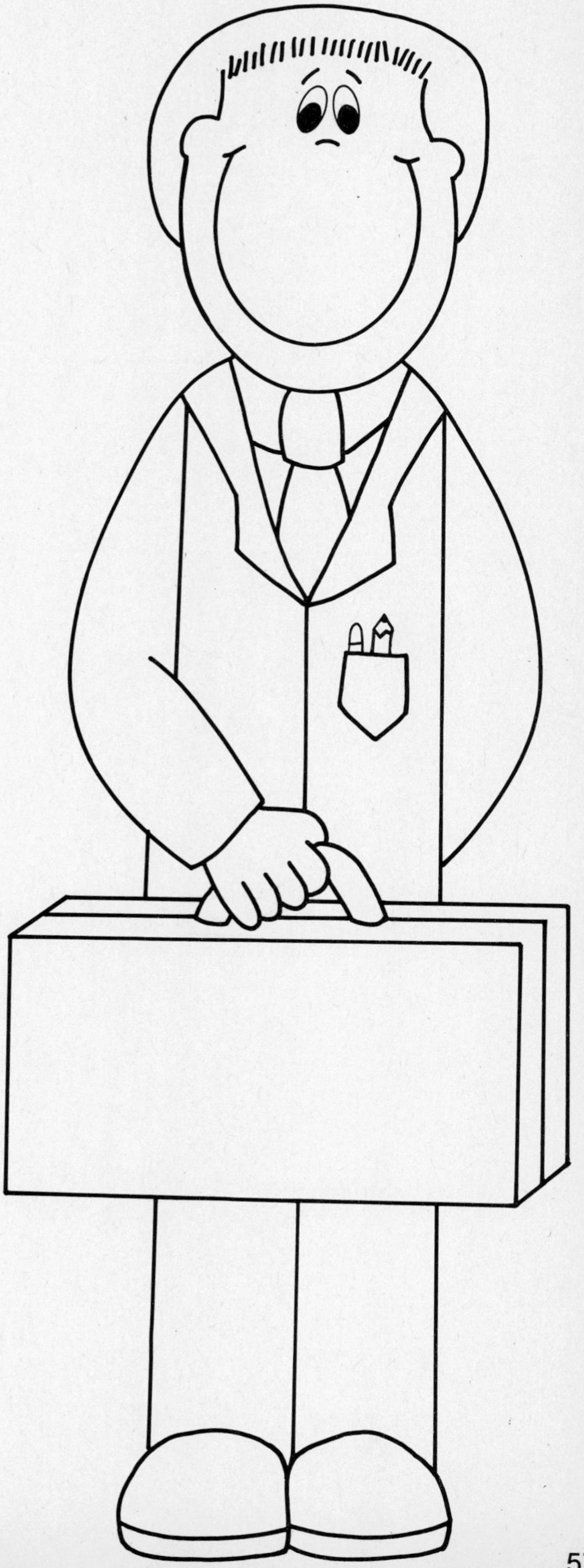

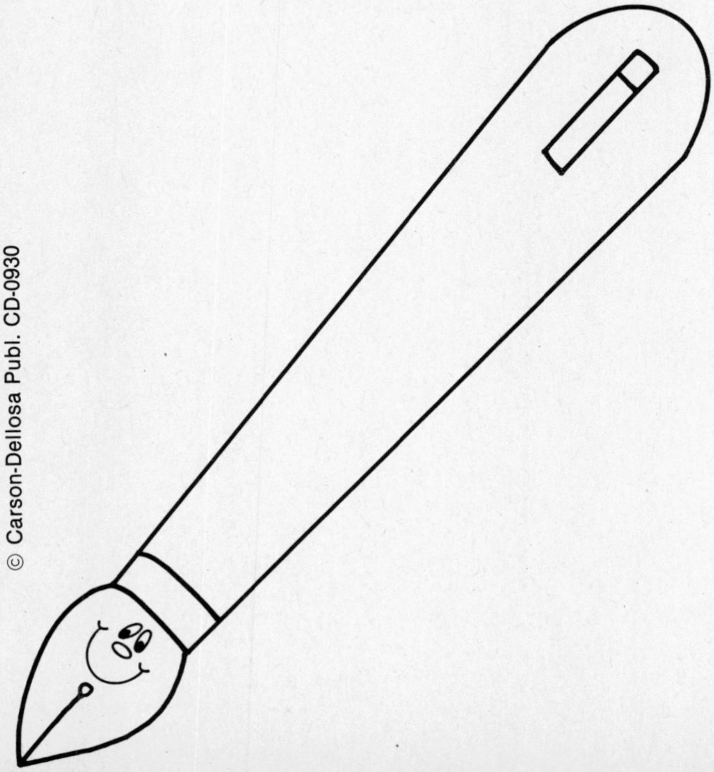

60

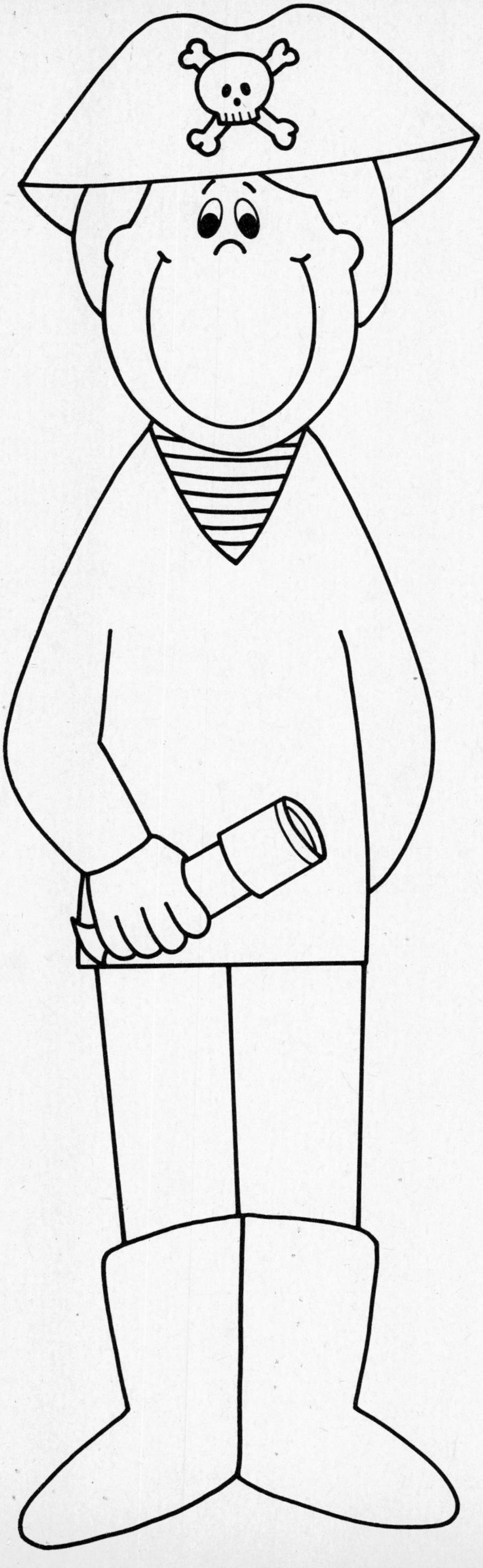

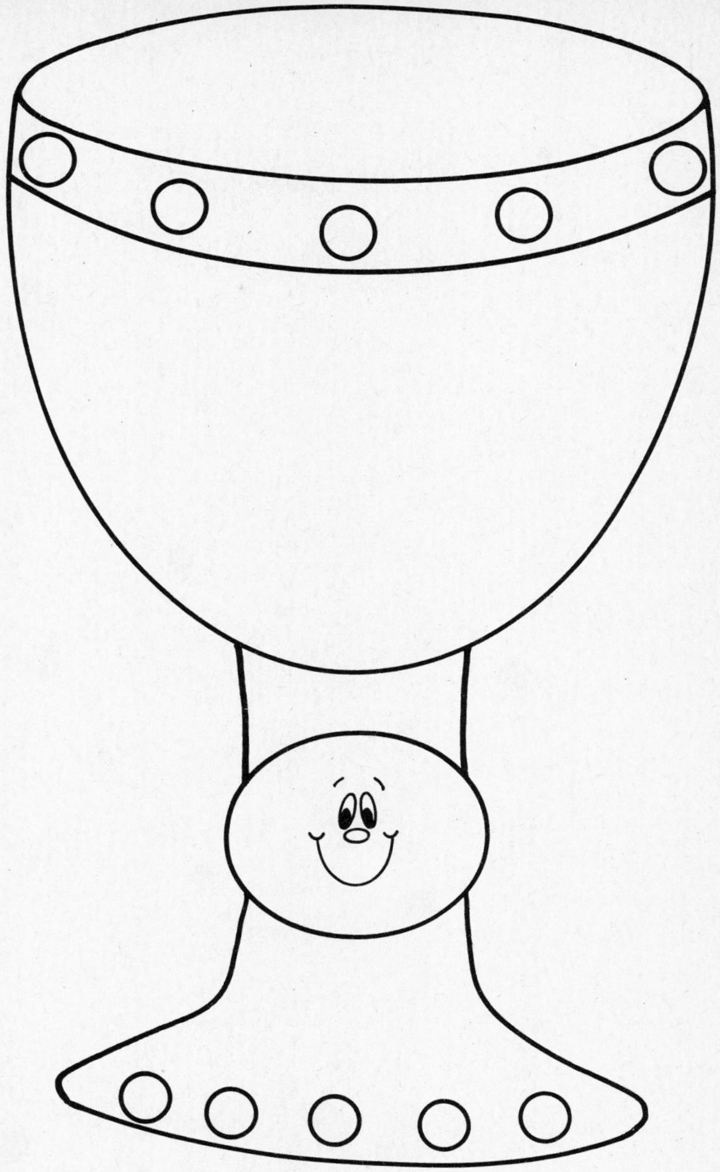

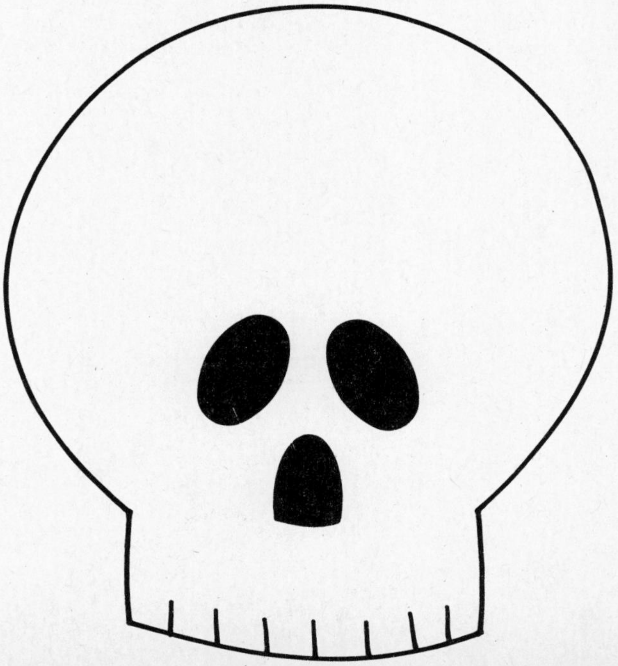

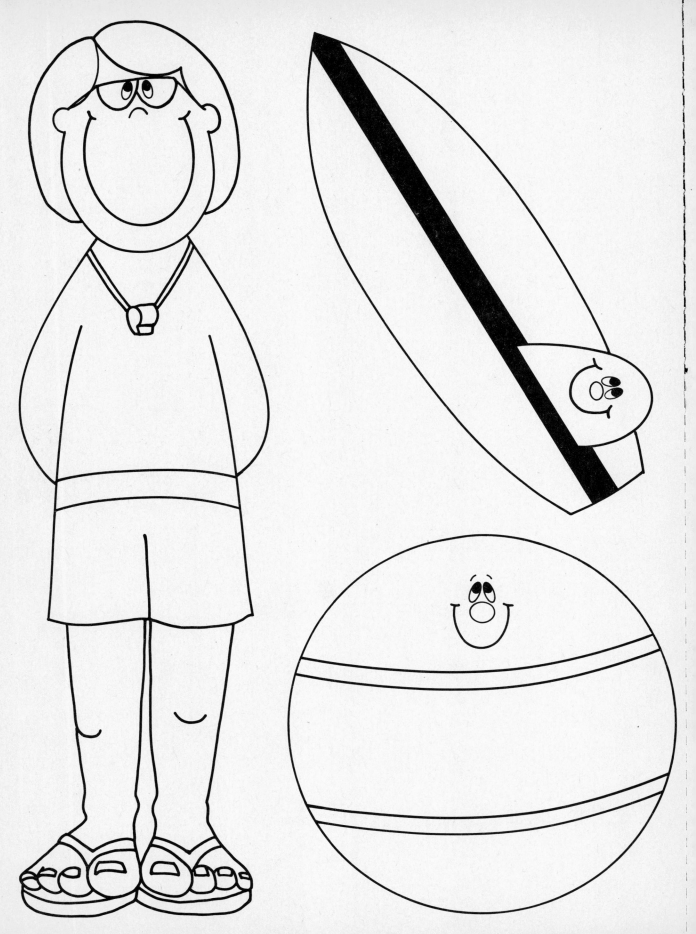

64

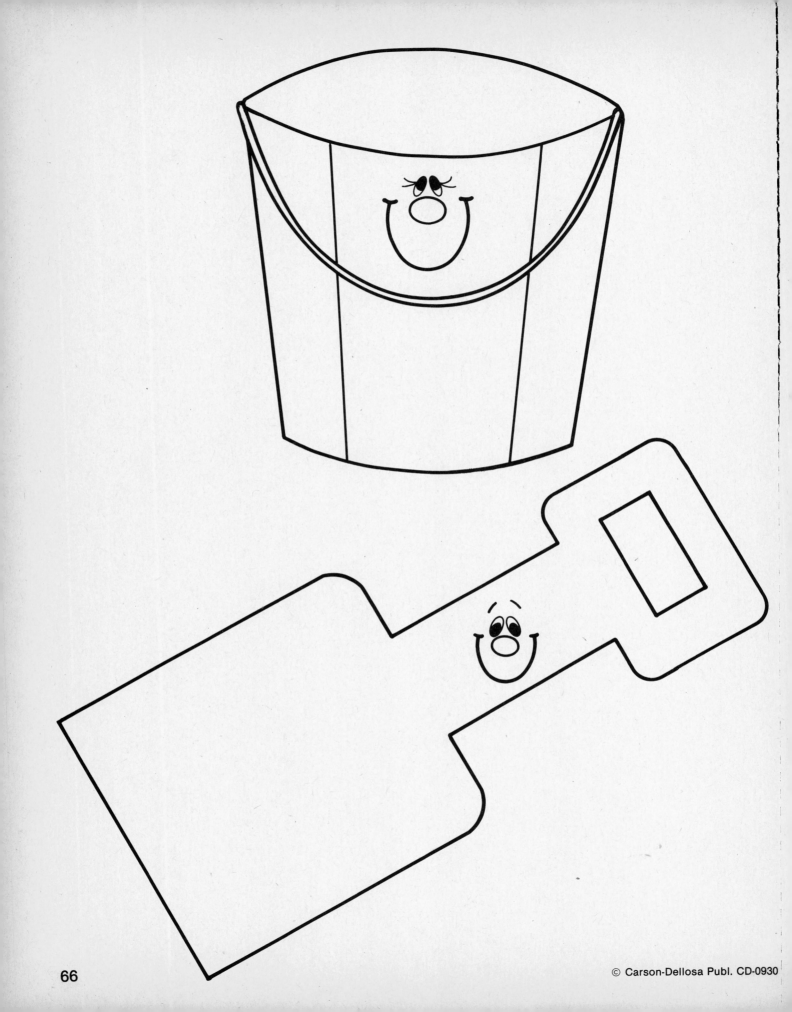

66

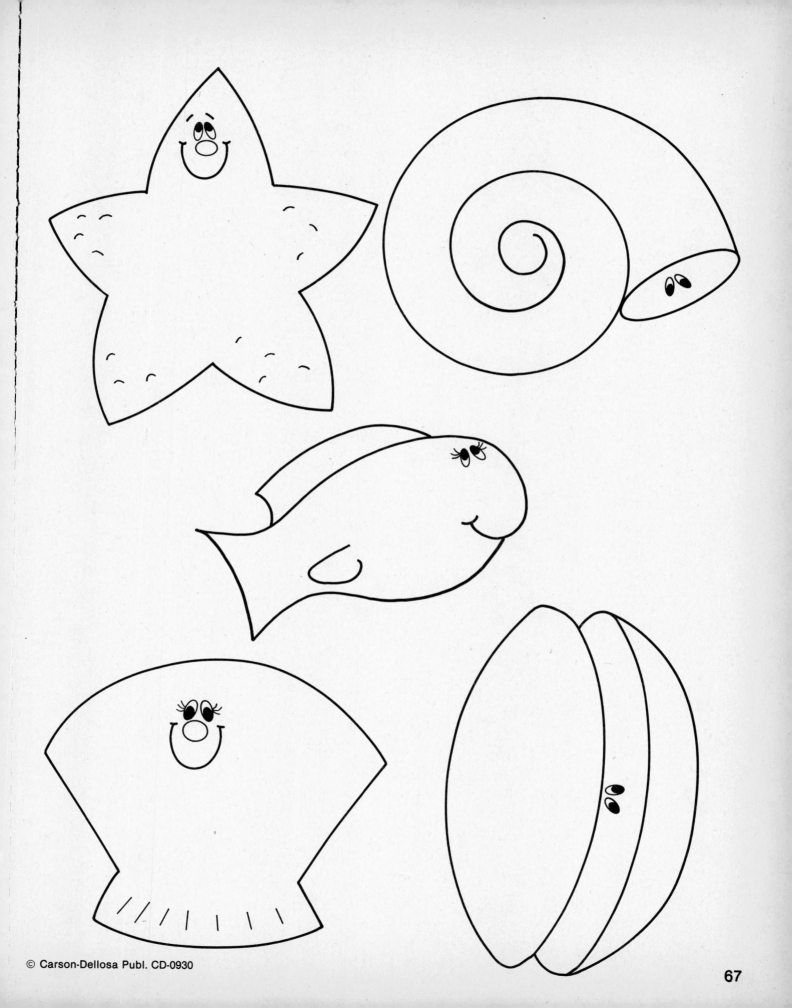

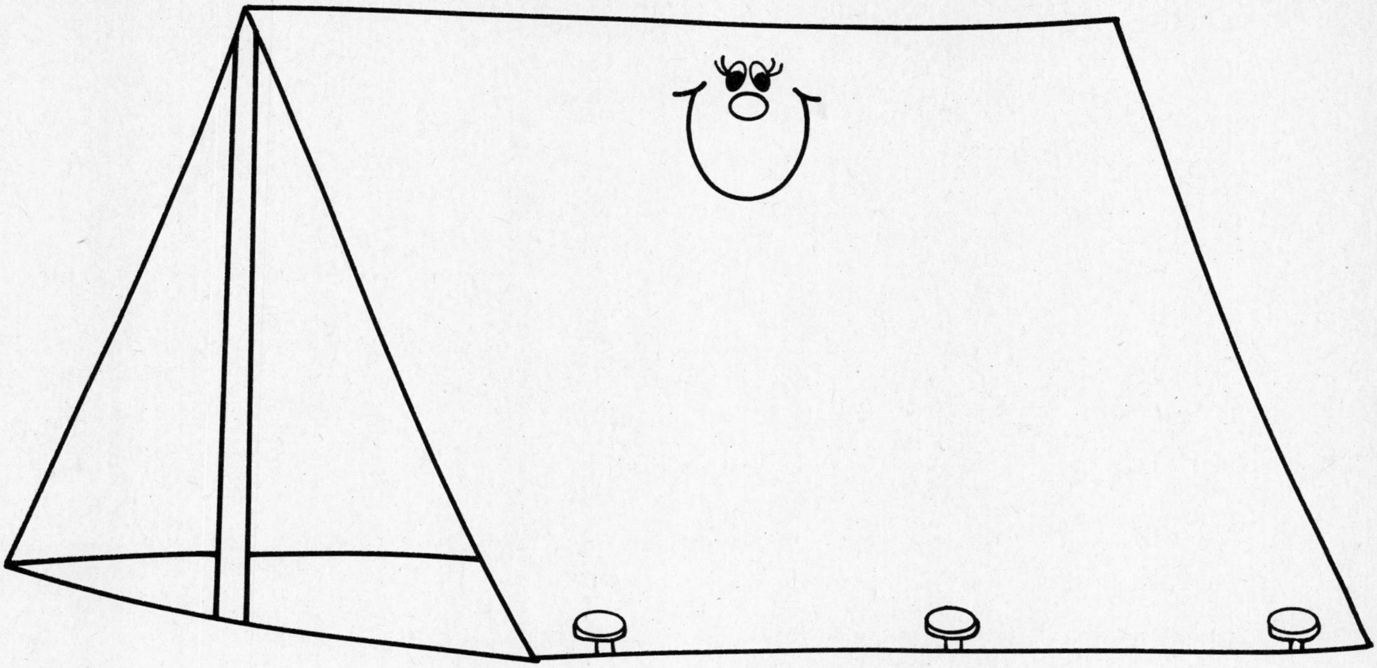

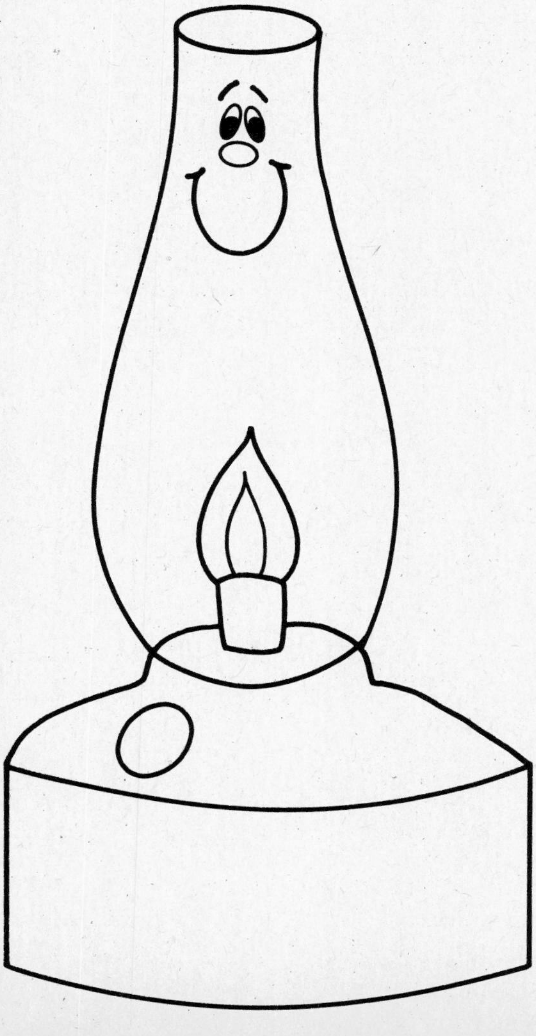

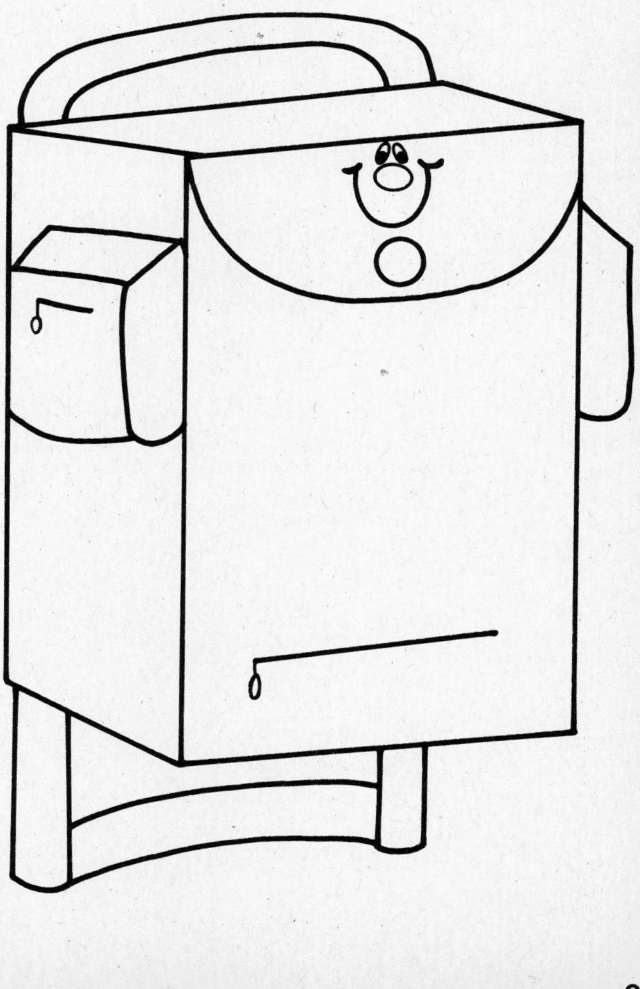

70

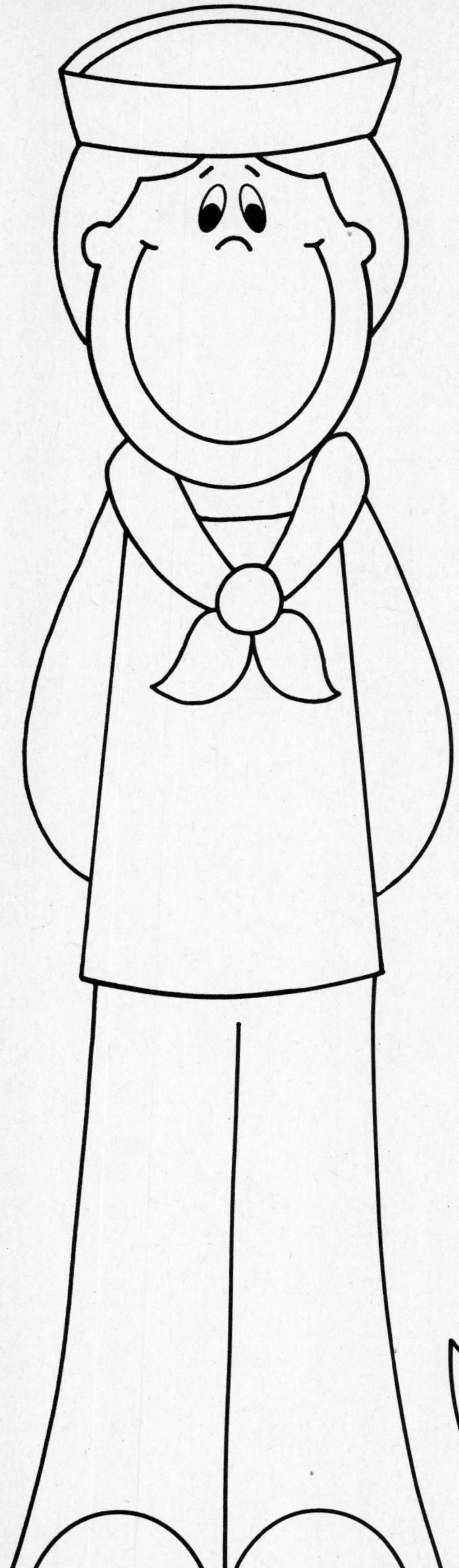

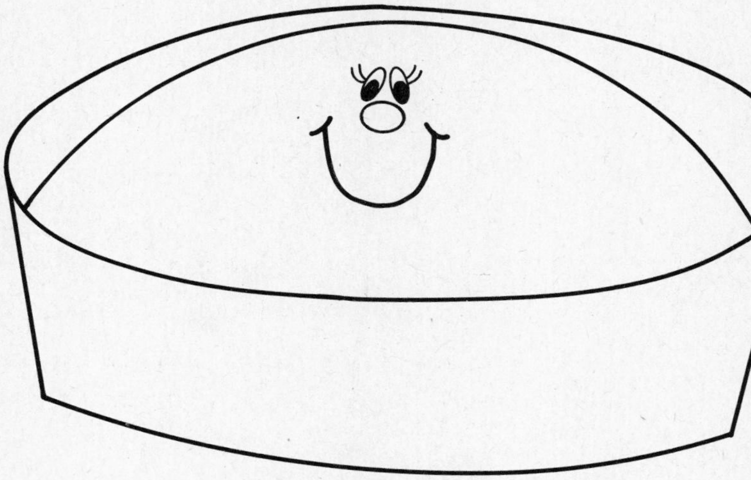

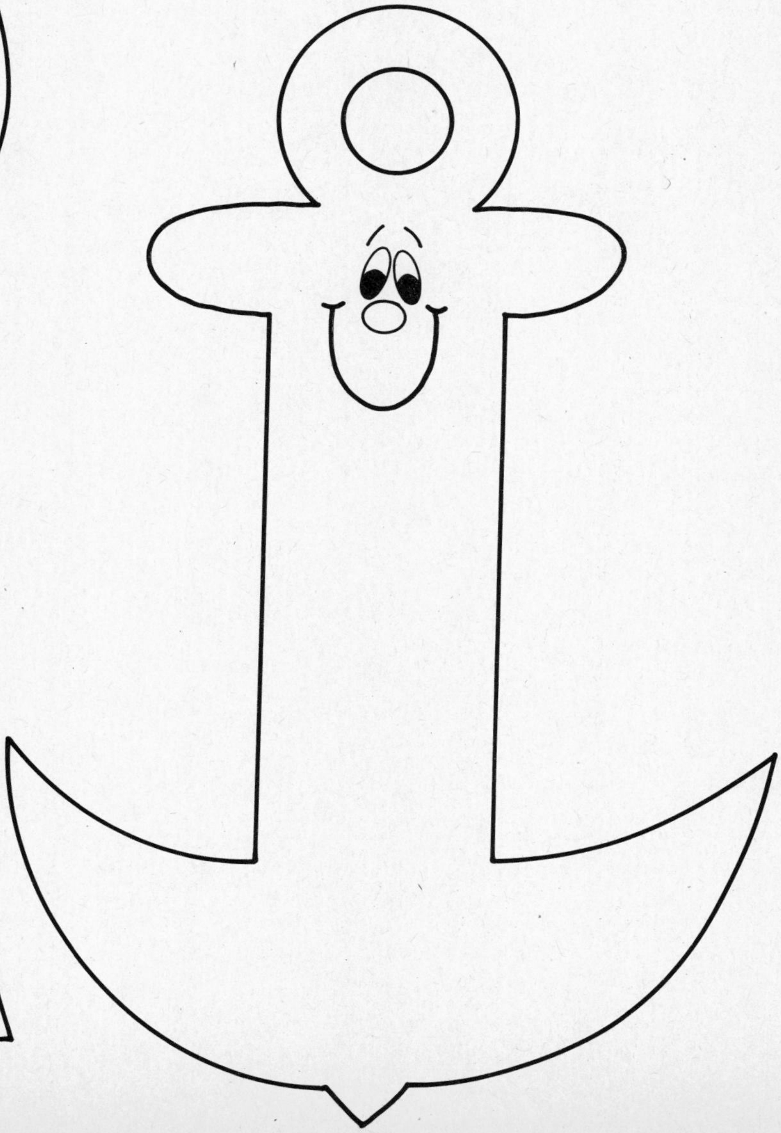

72

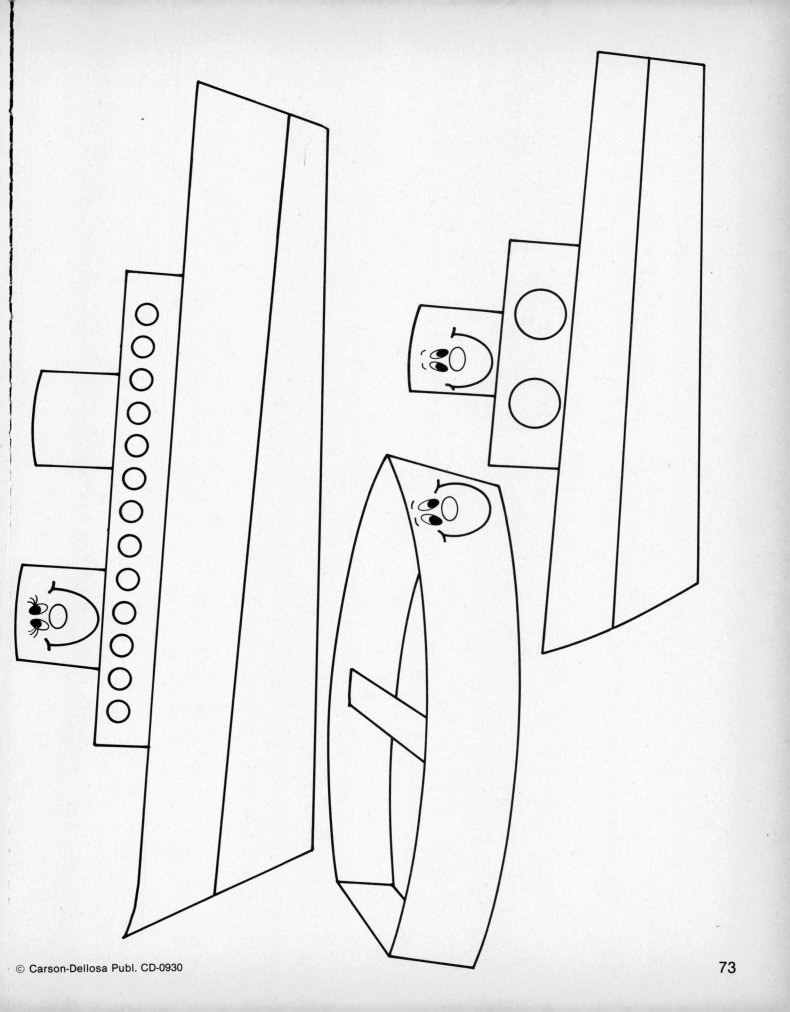

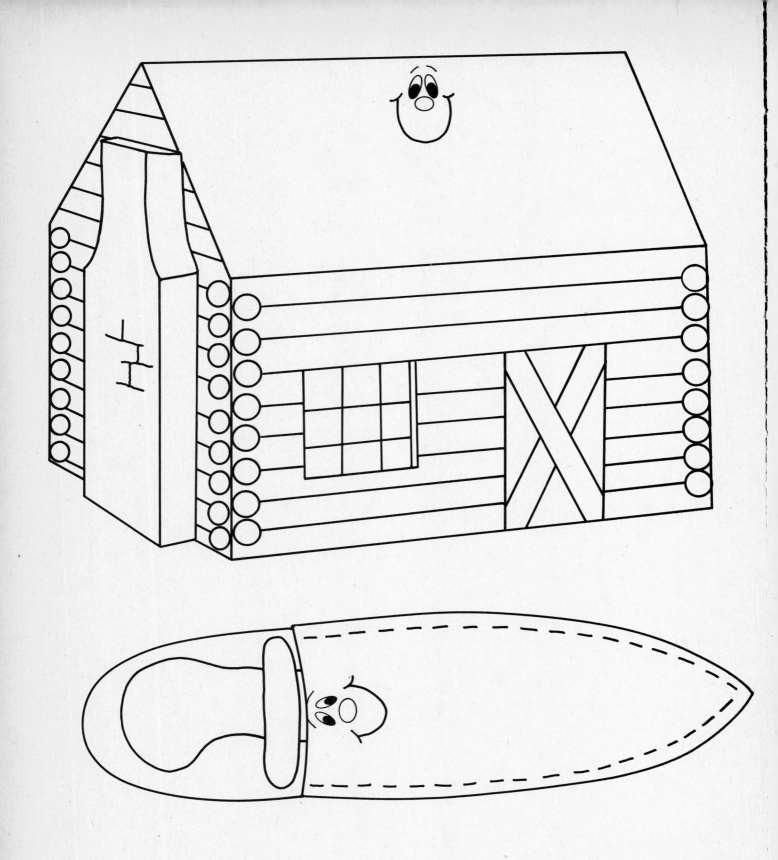

74

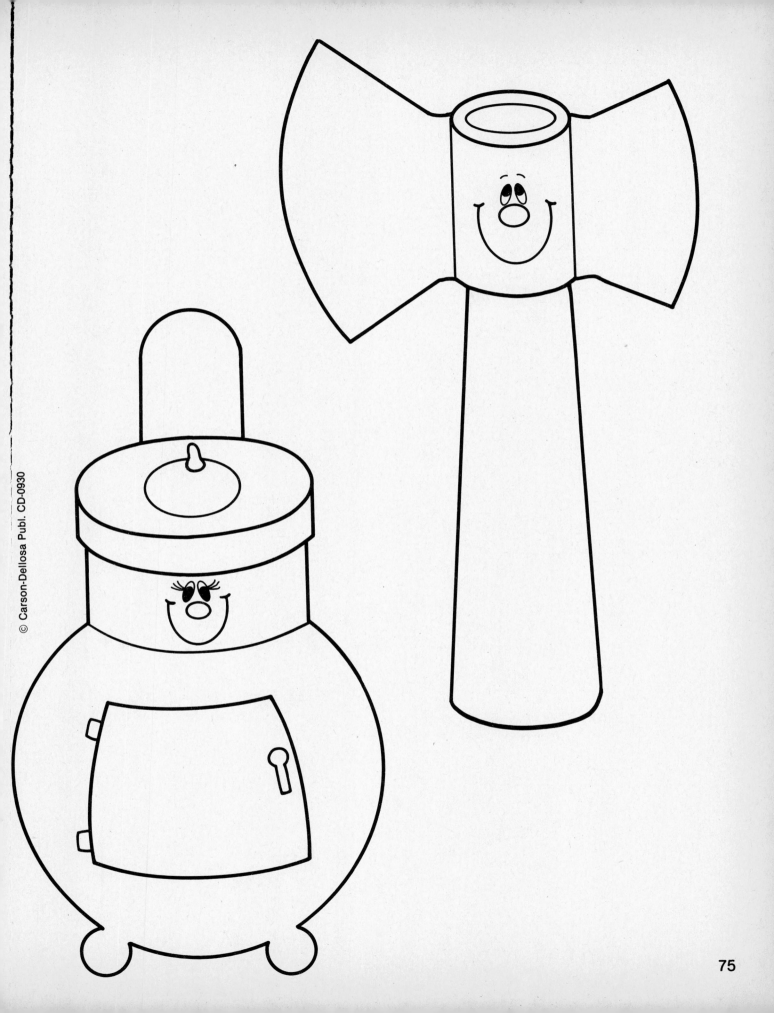

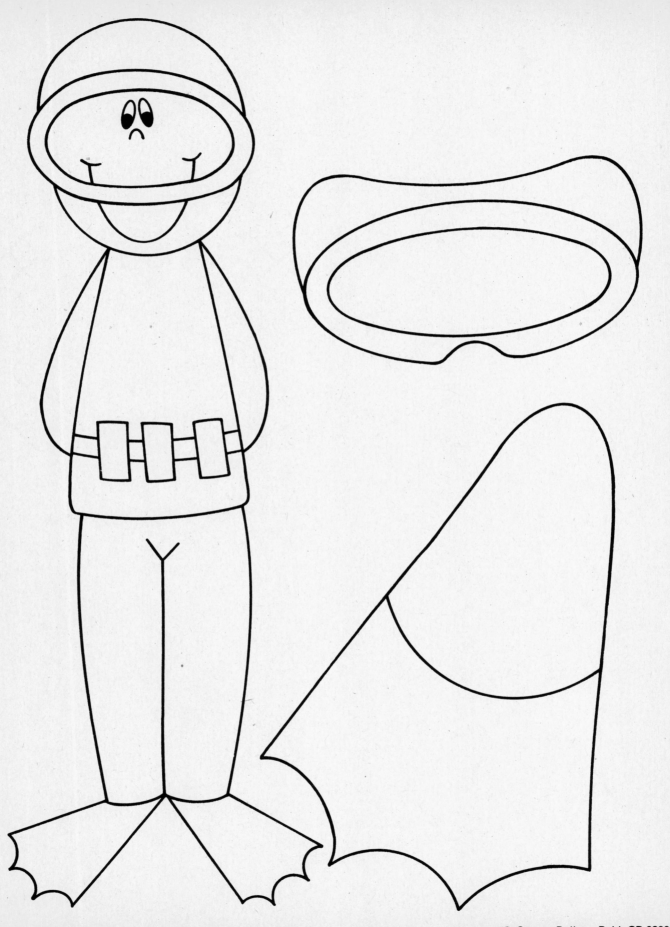

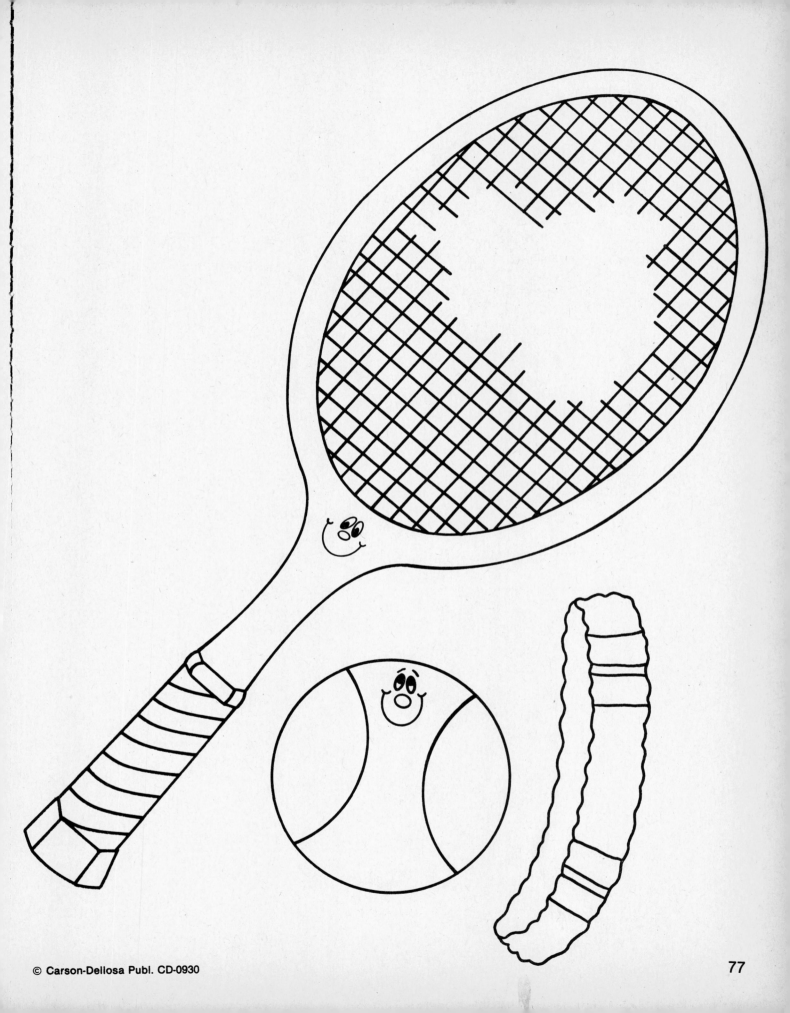

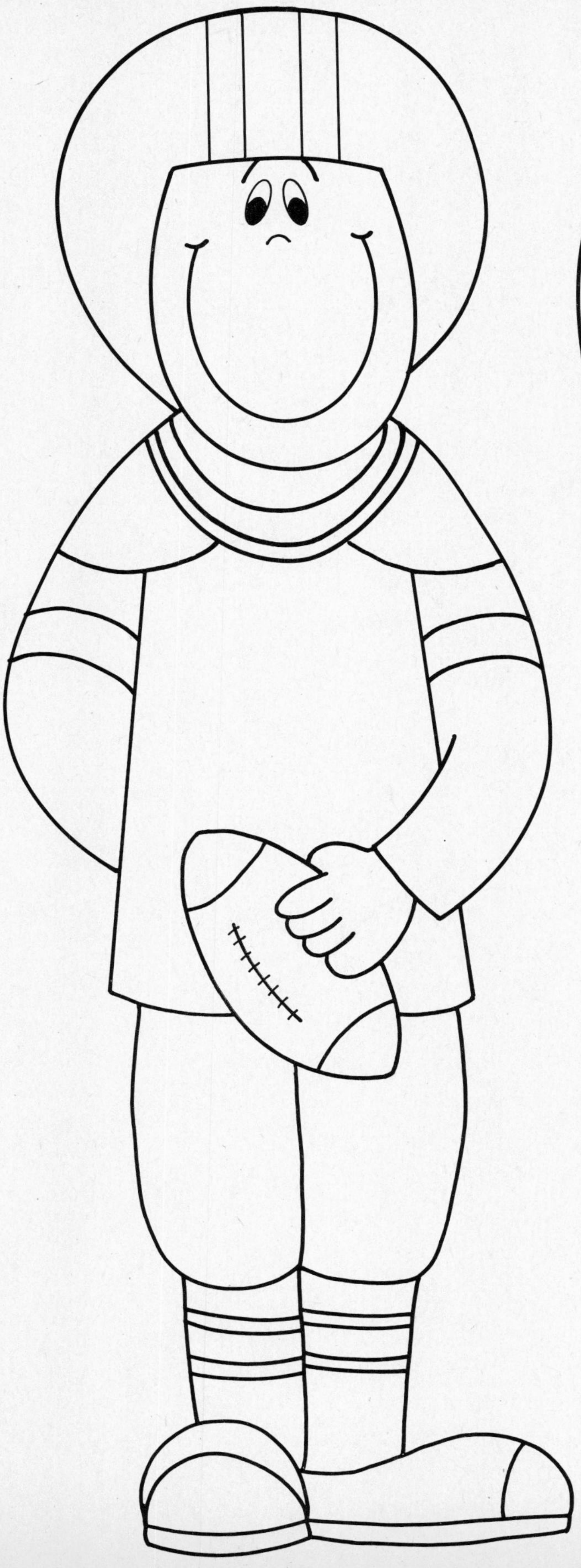

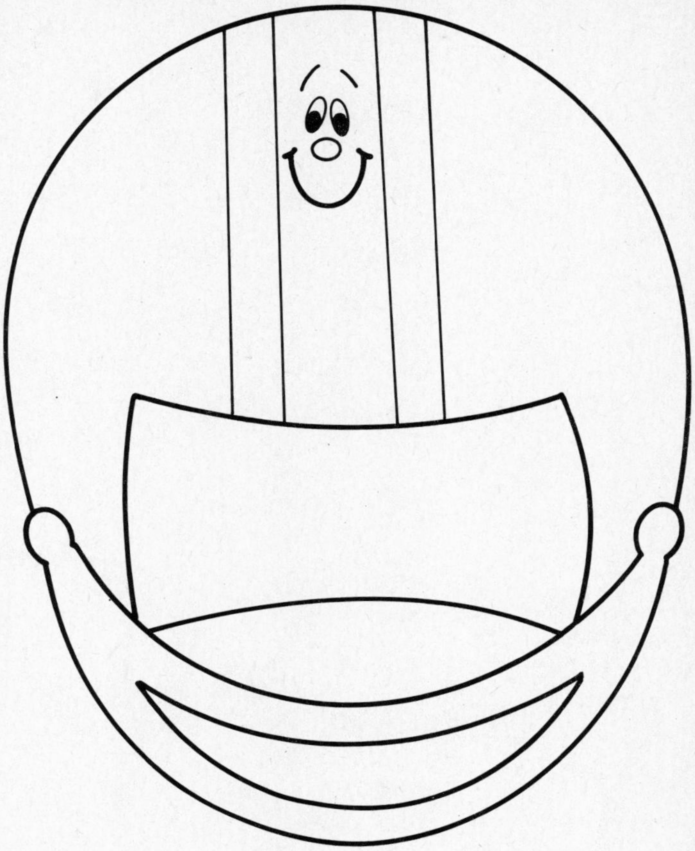

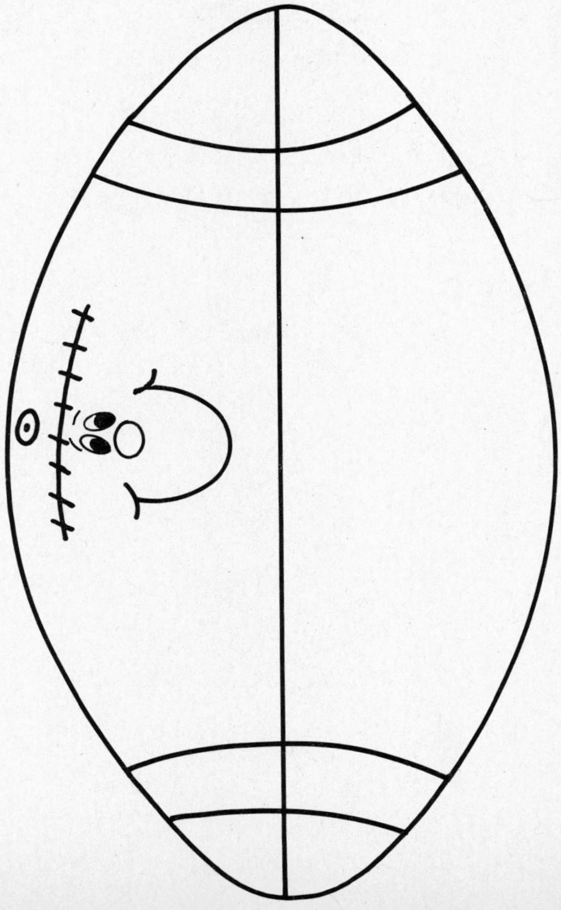

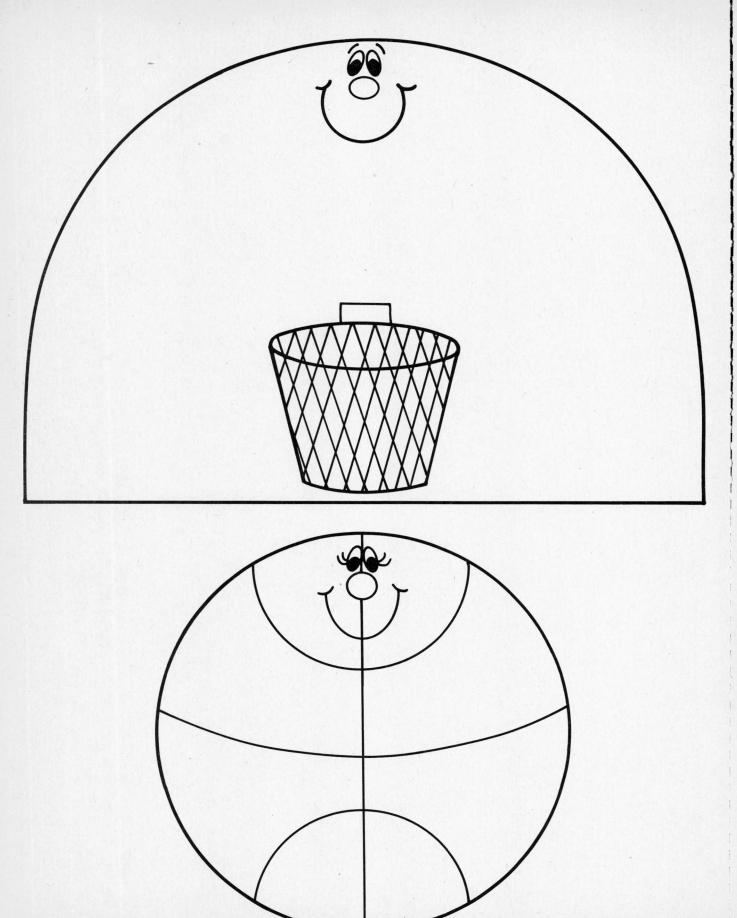

82

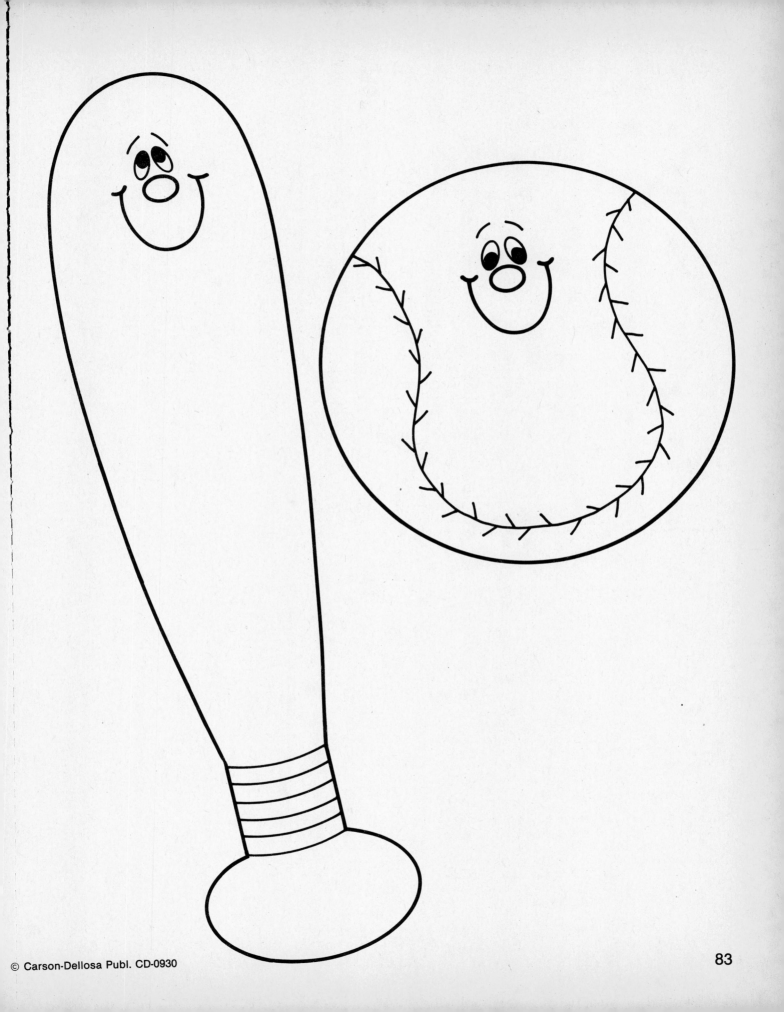

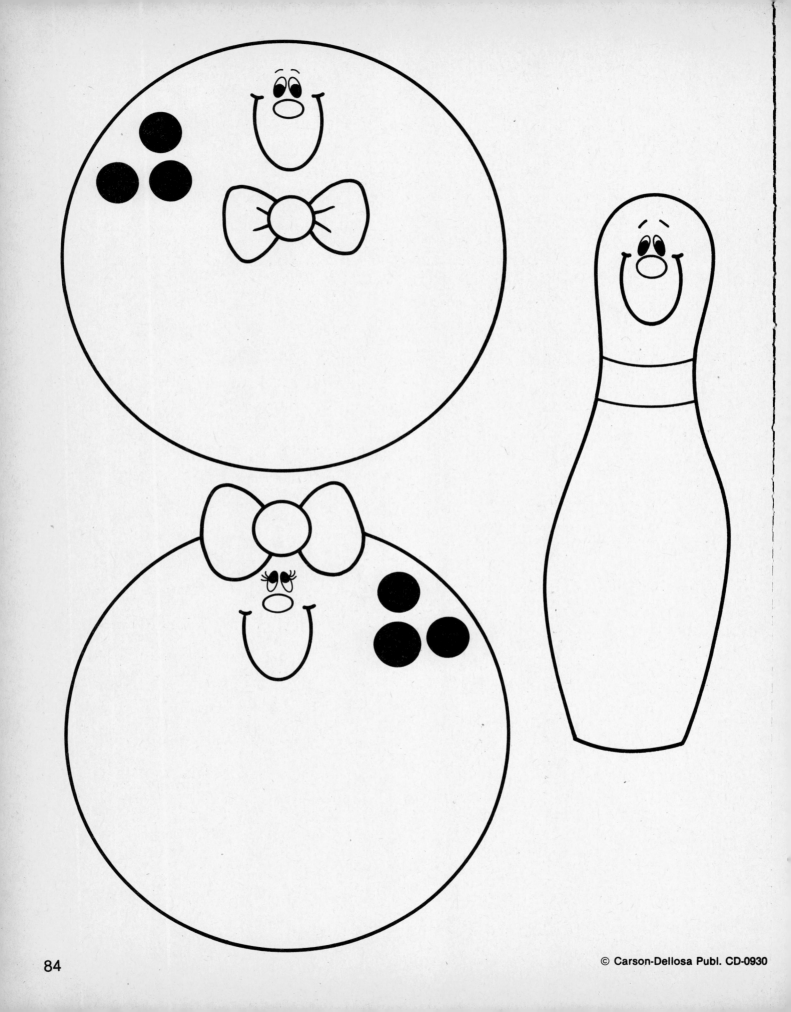

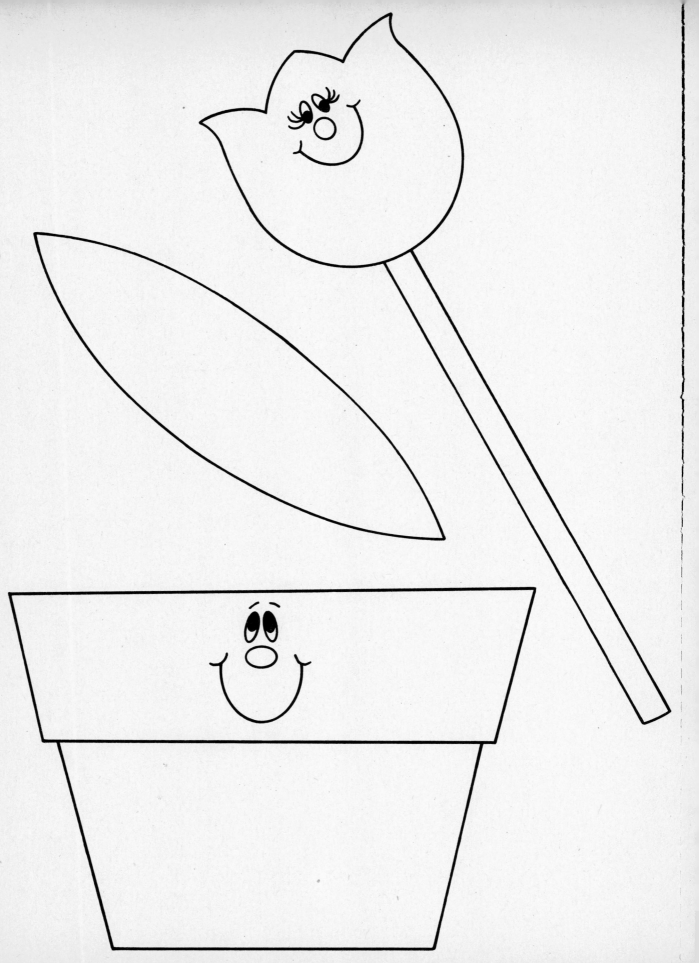

86

88

90

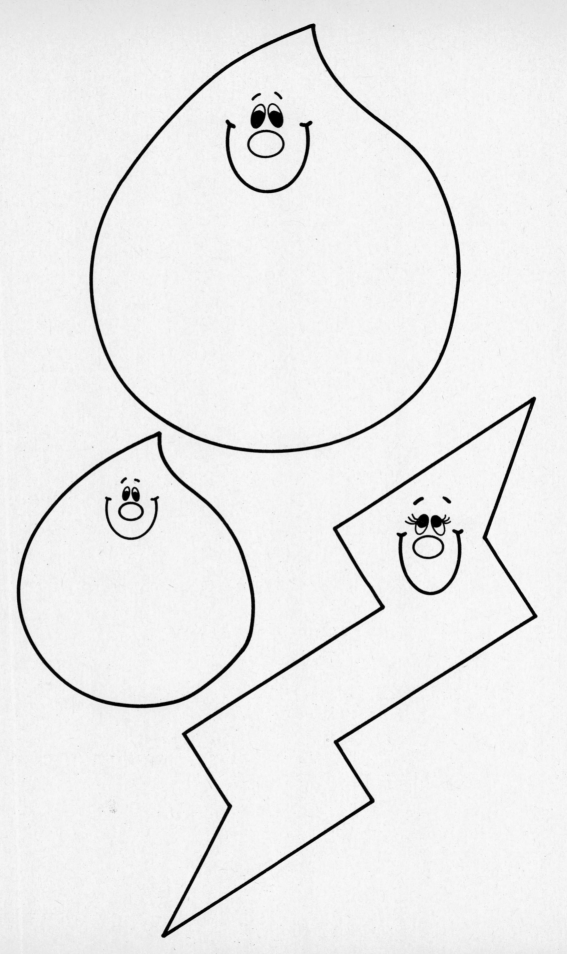

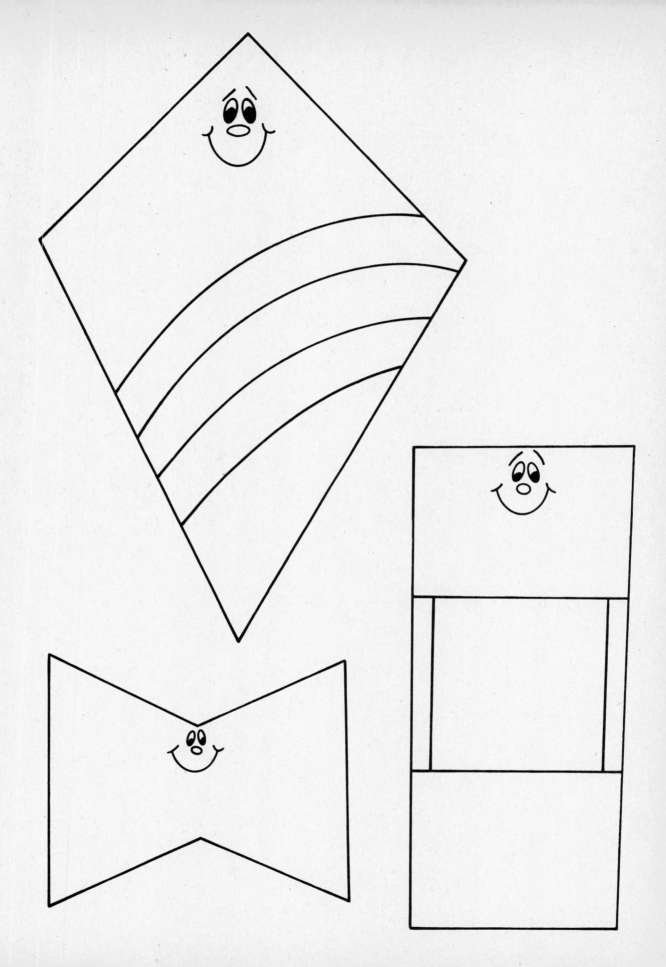

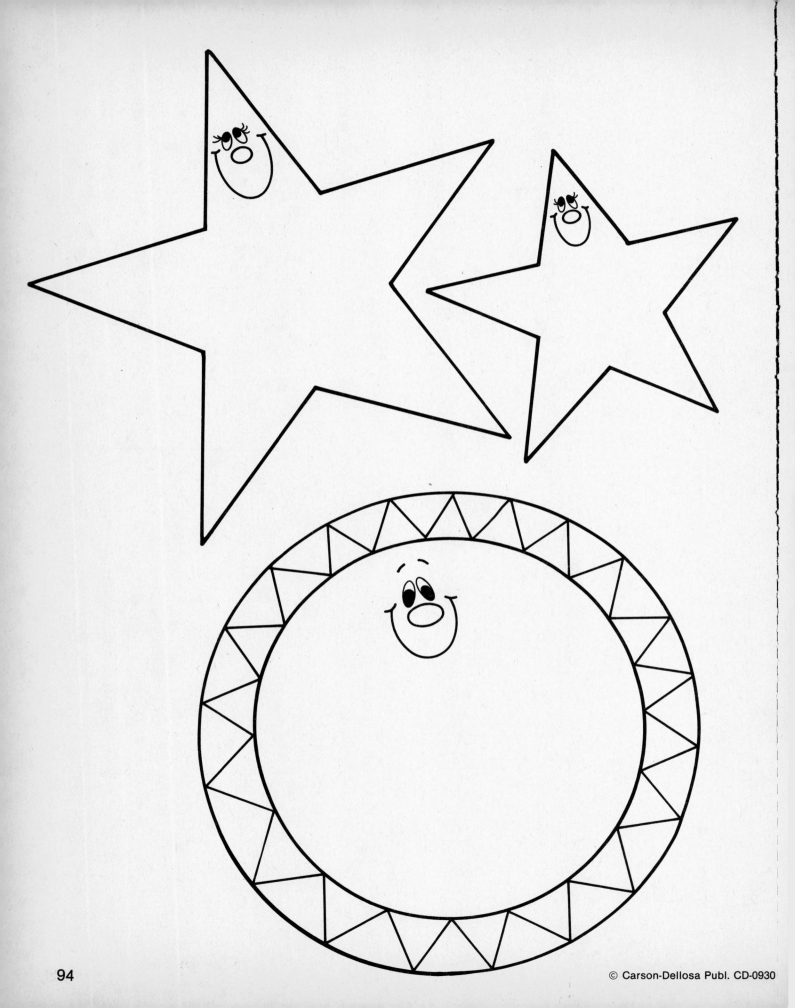

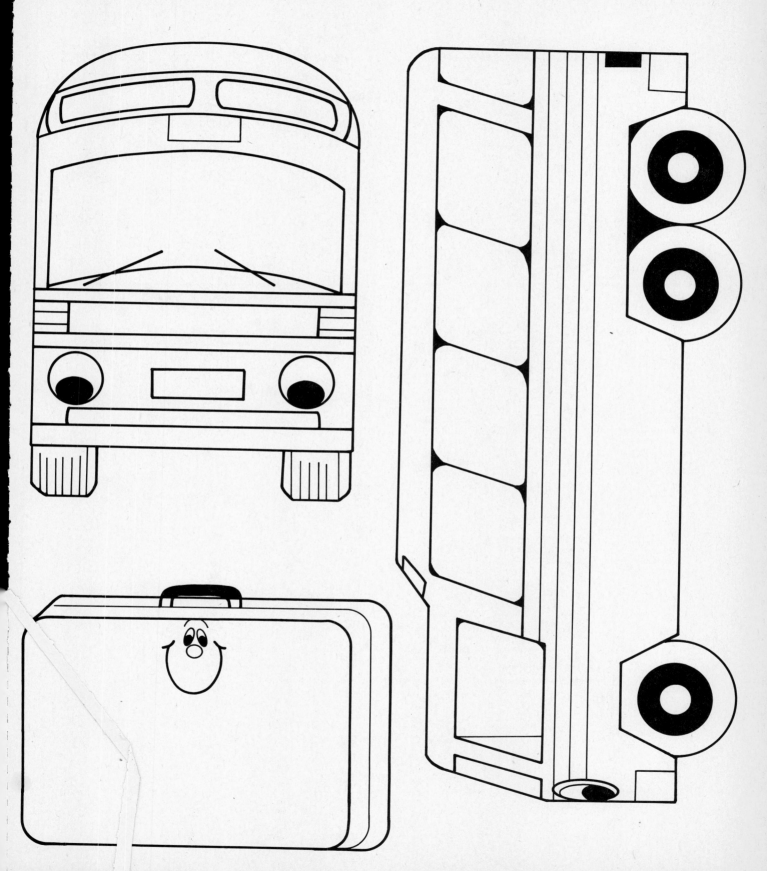

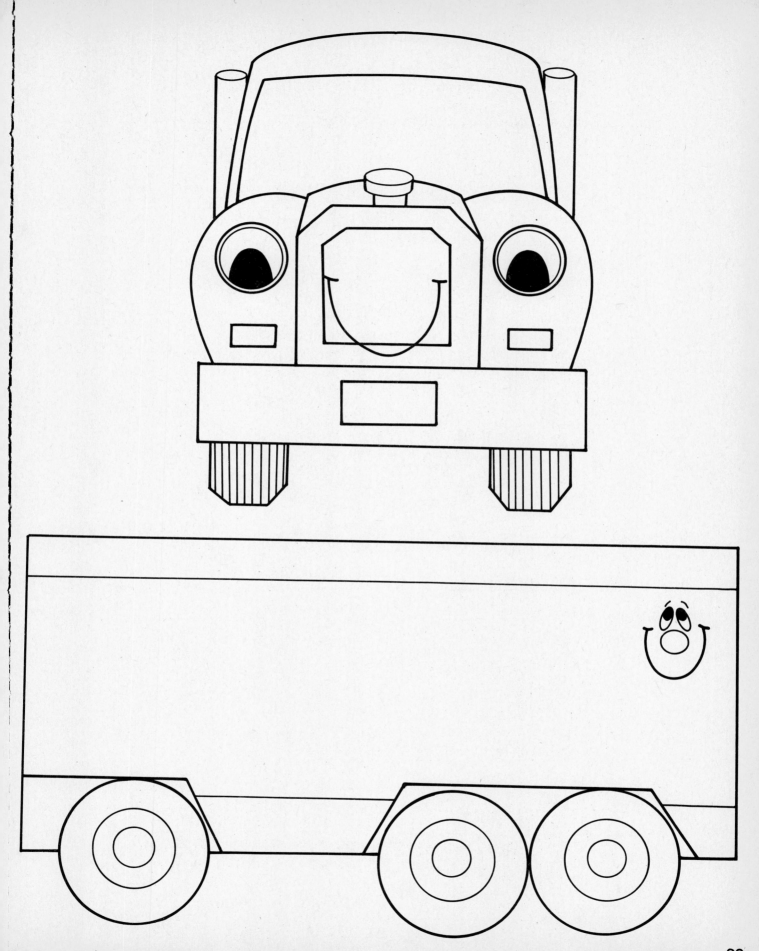

100

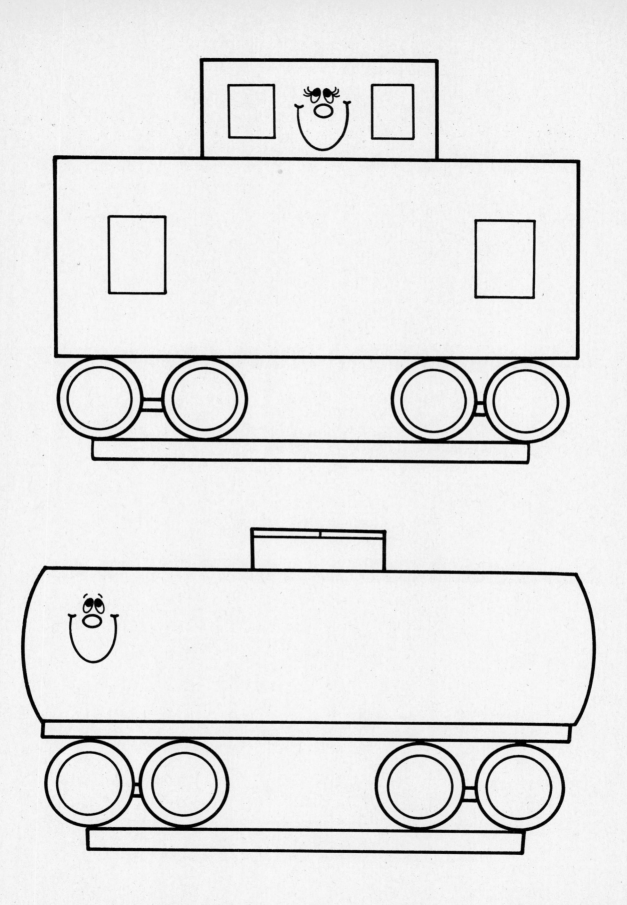

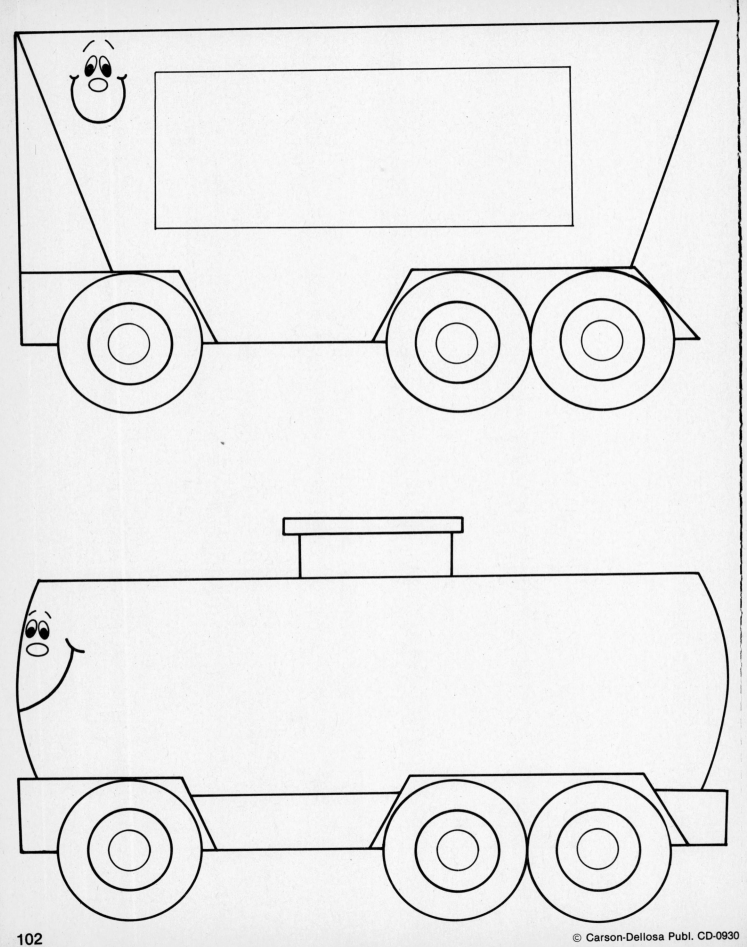

102

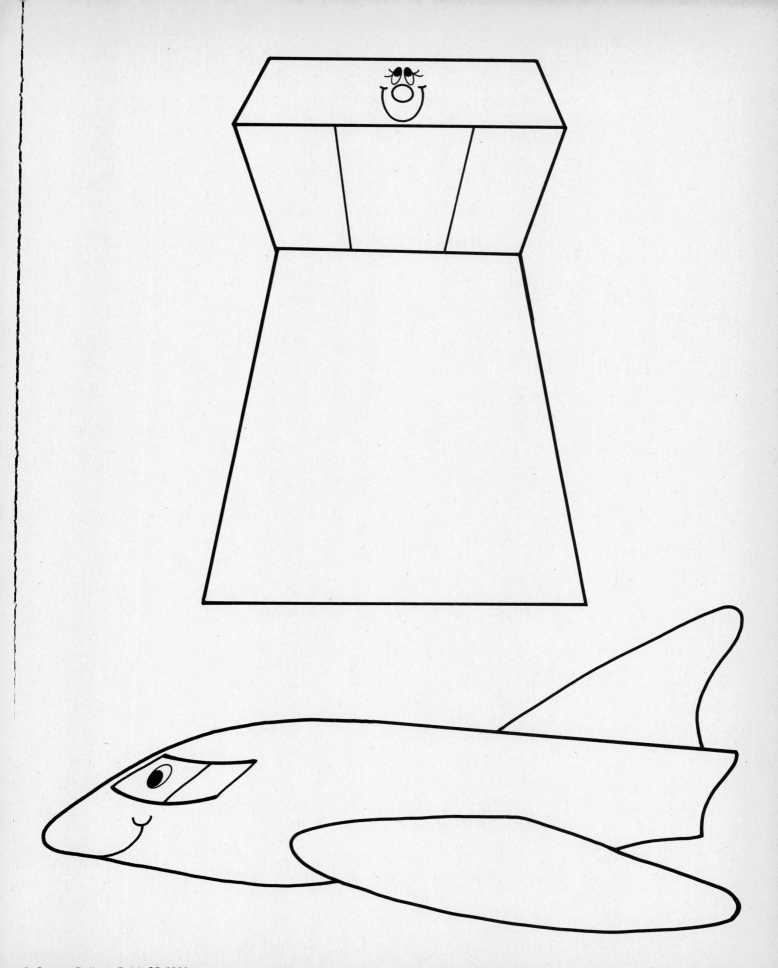

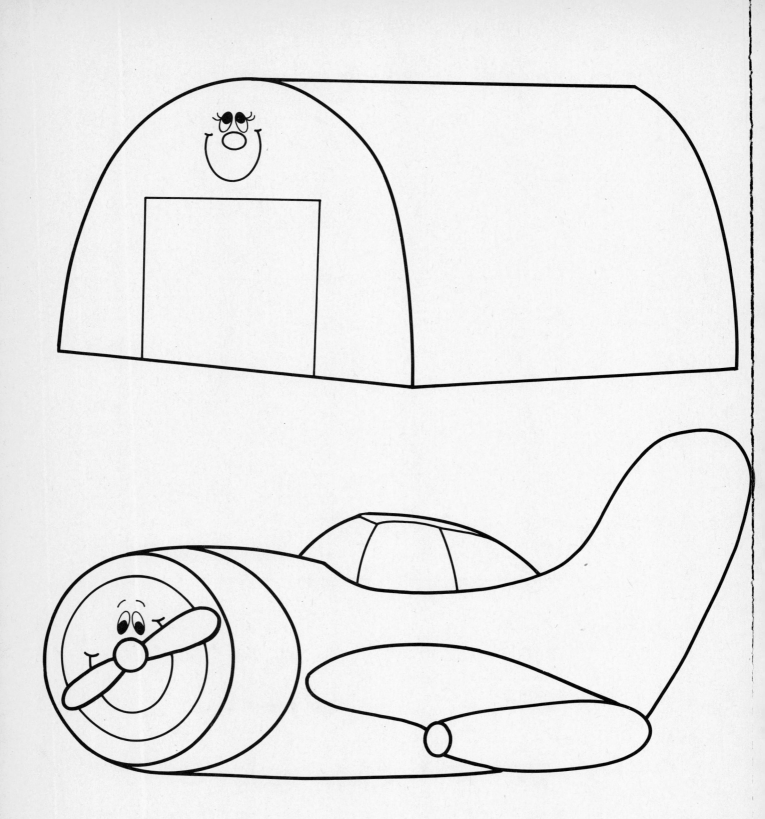

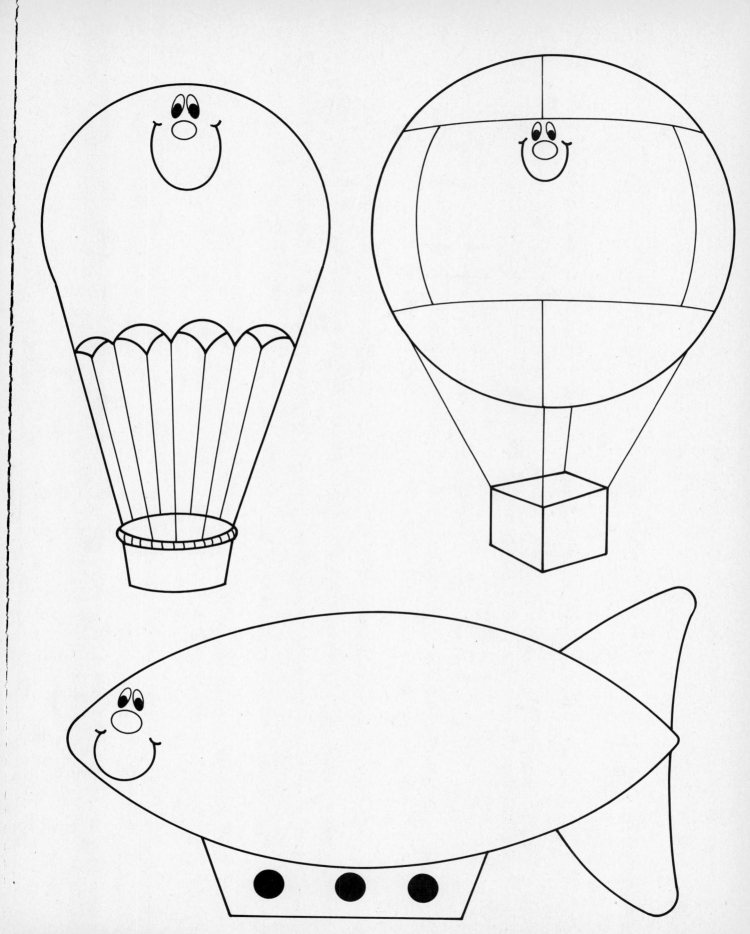

106

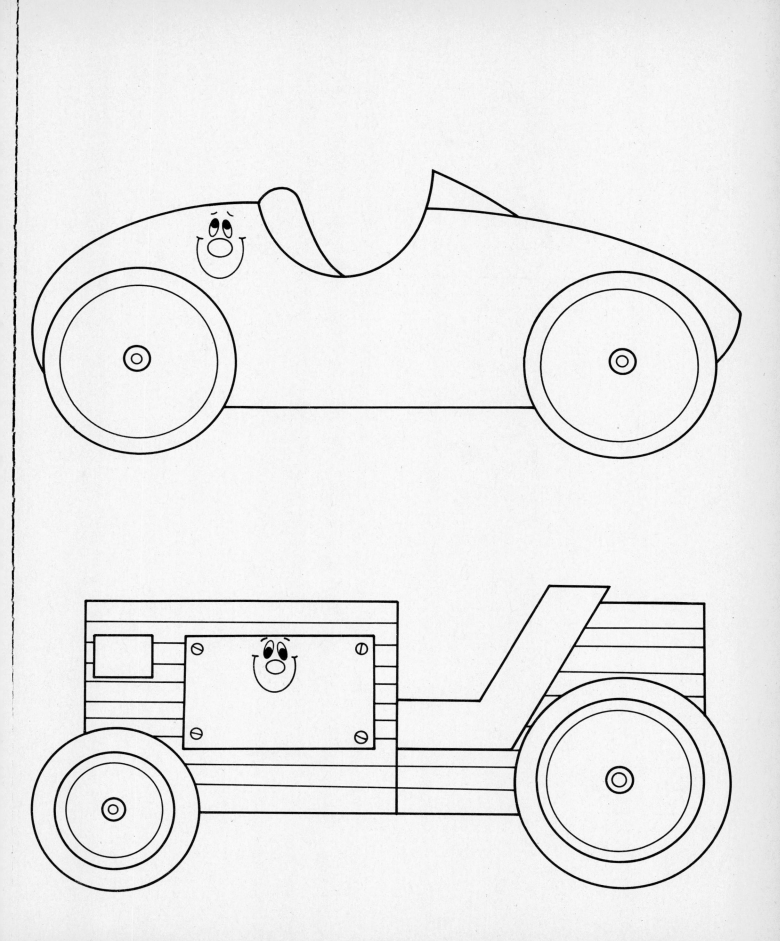

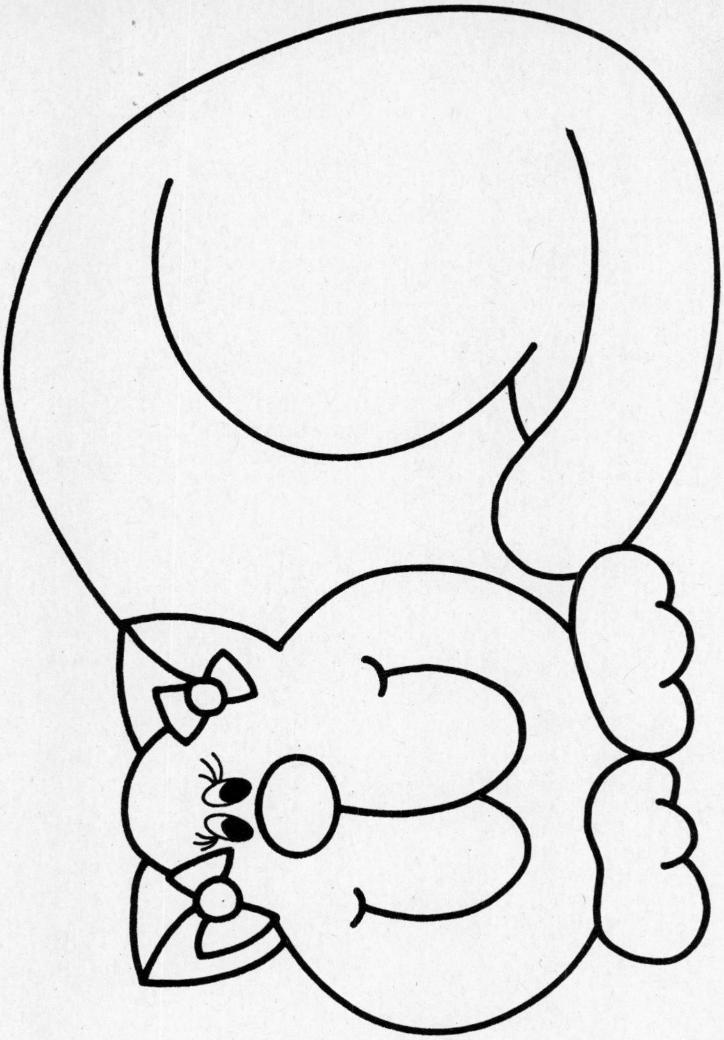

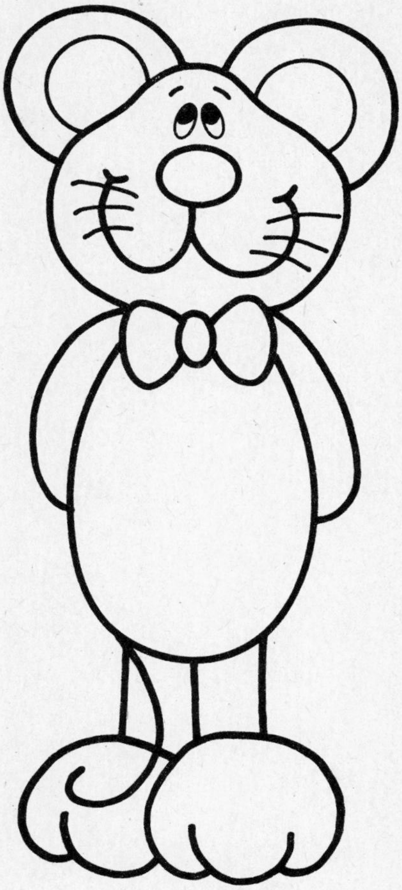

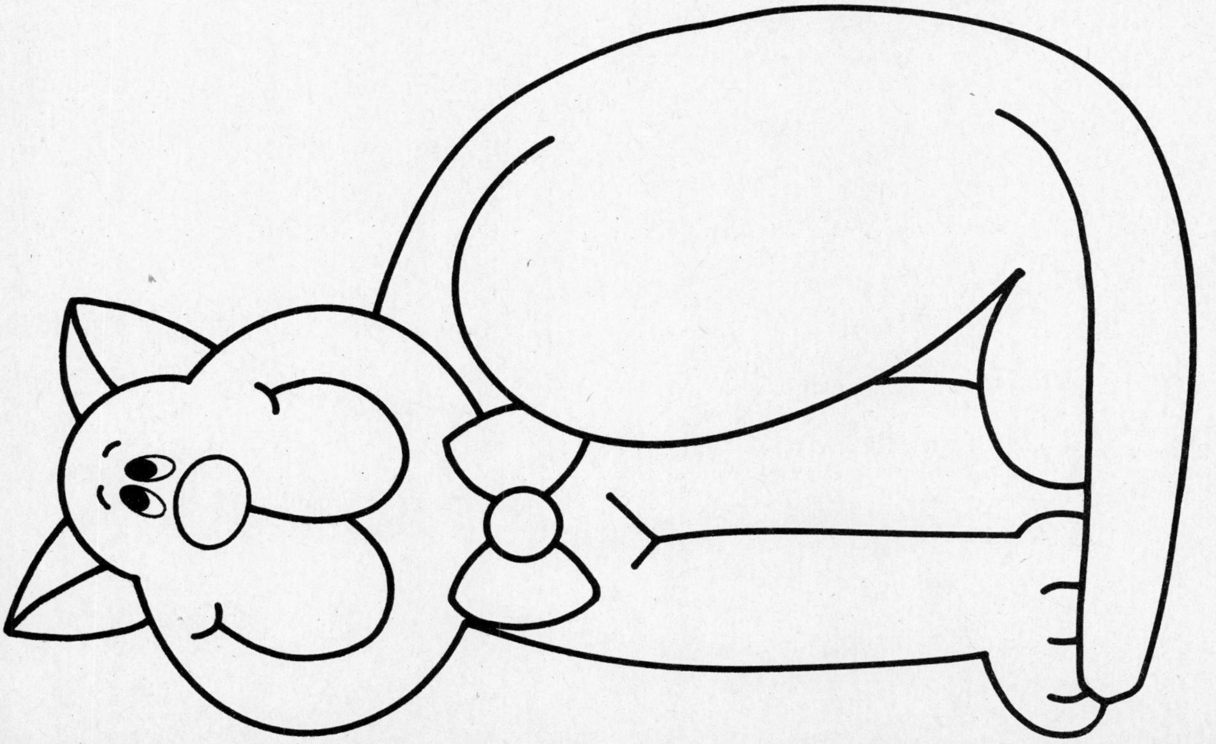

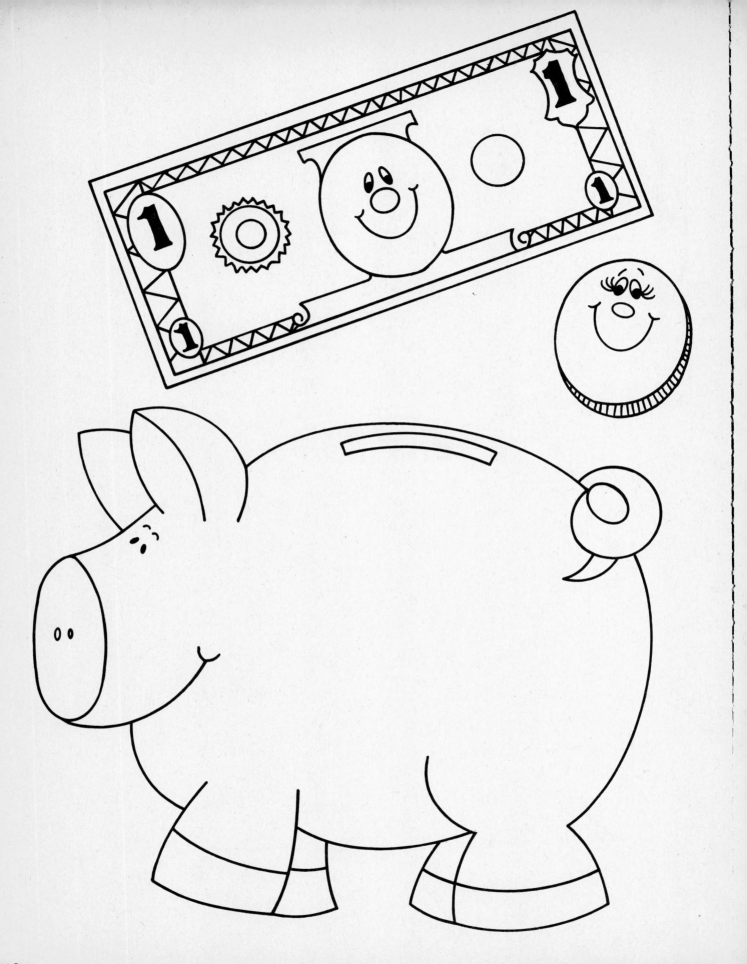

112

114

116

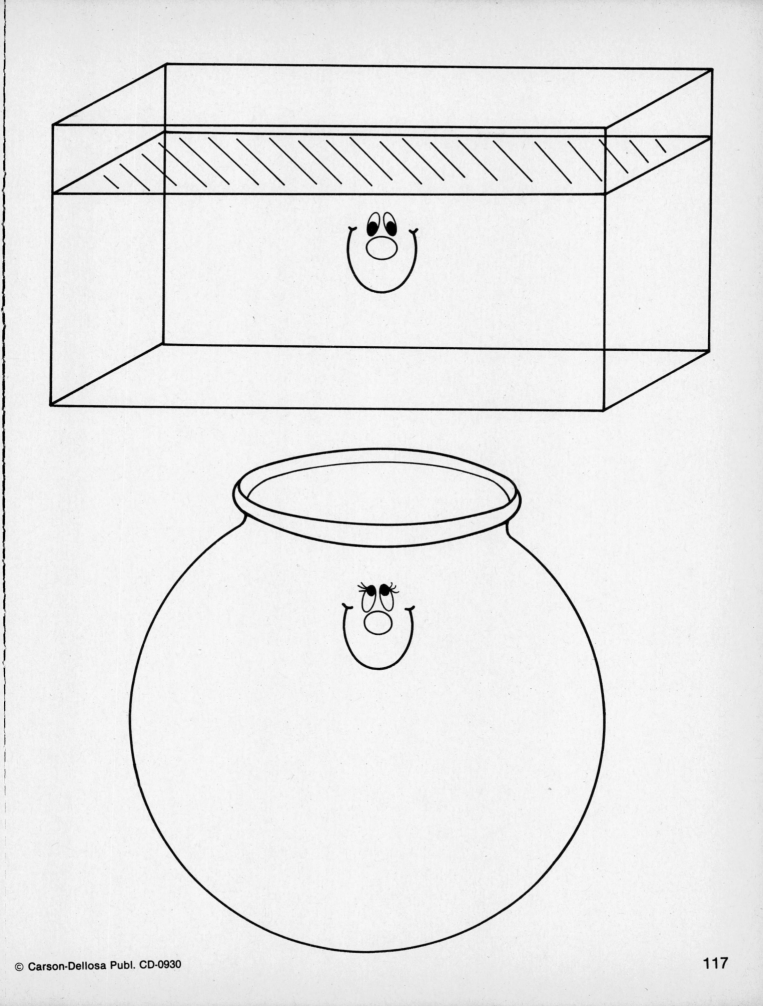

118

122

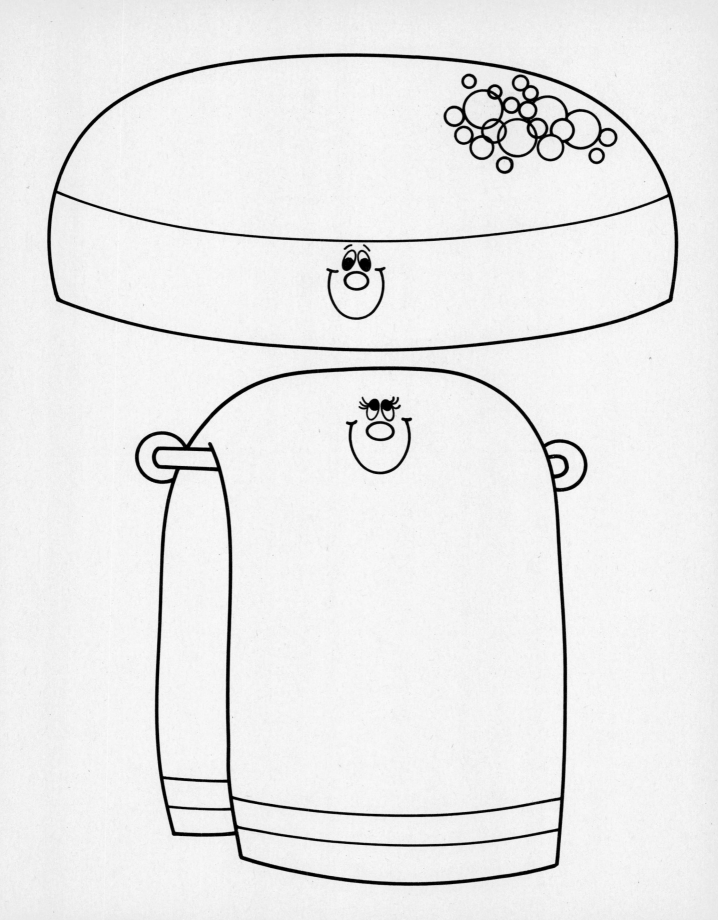

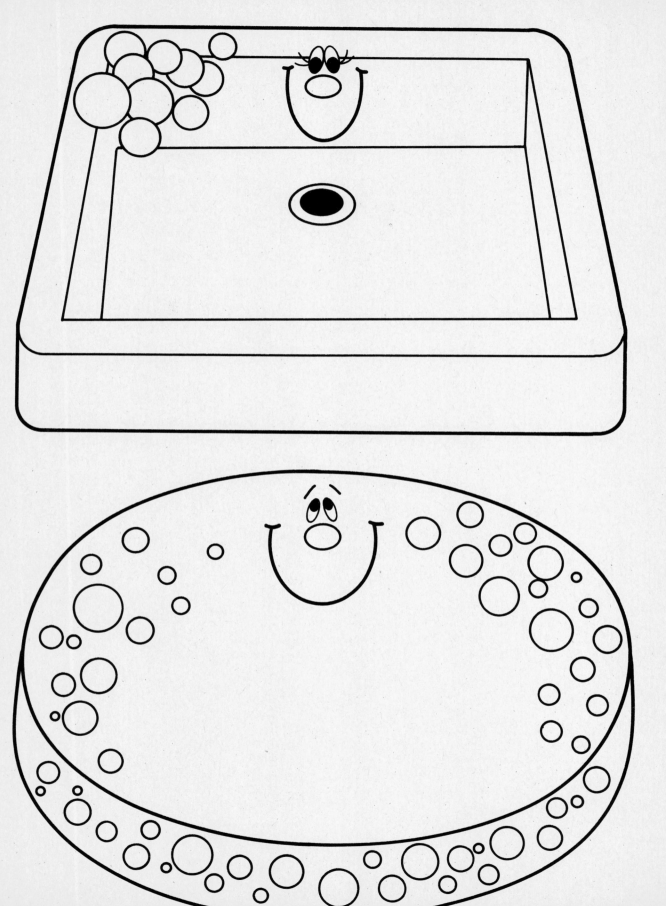

124

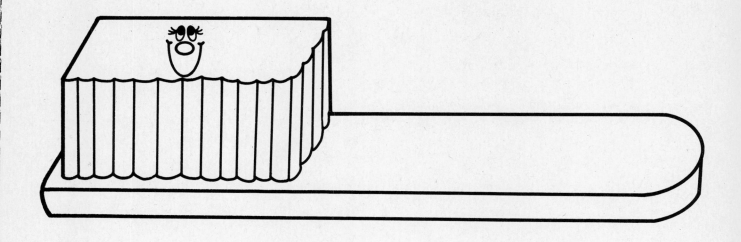

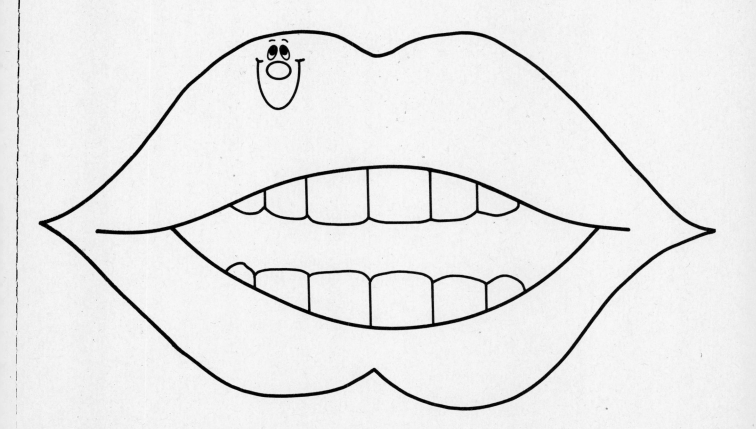

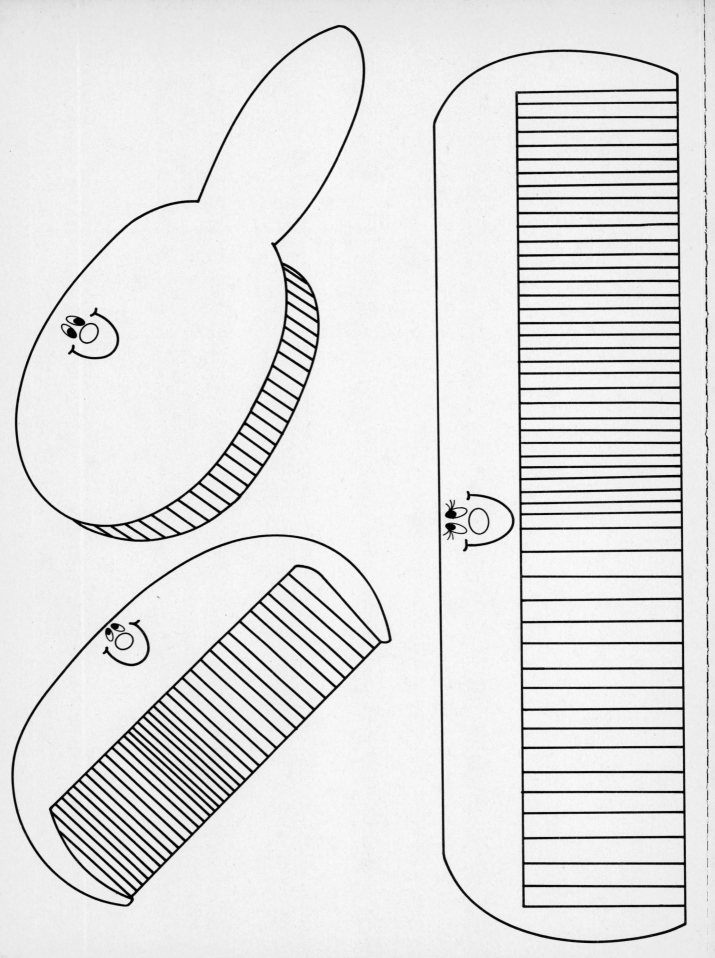

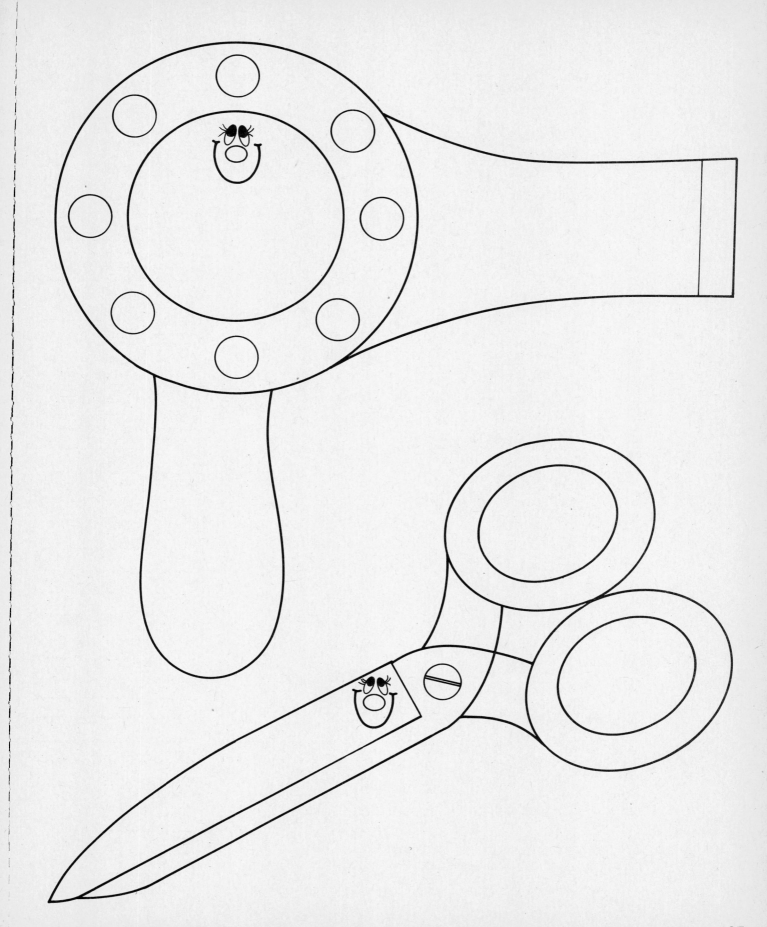

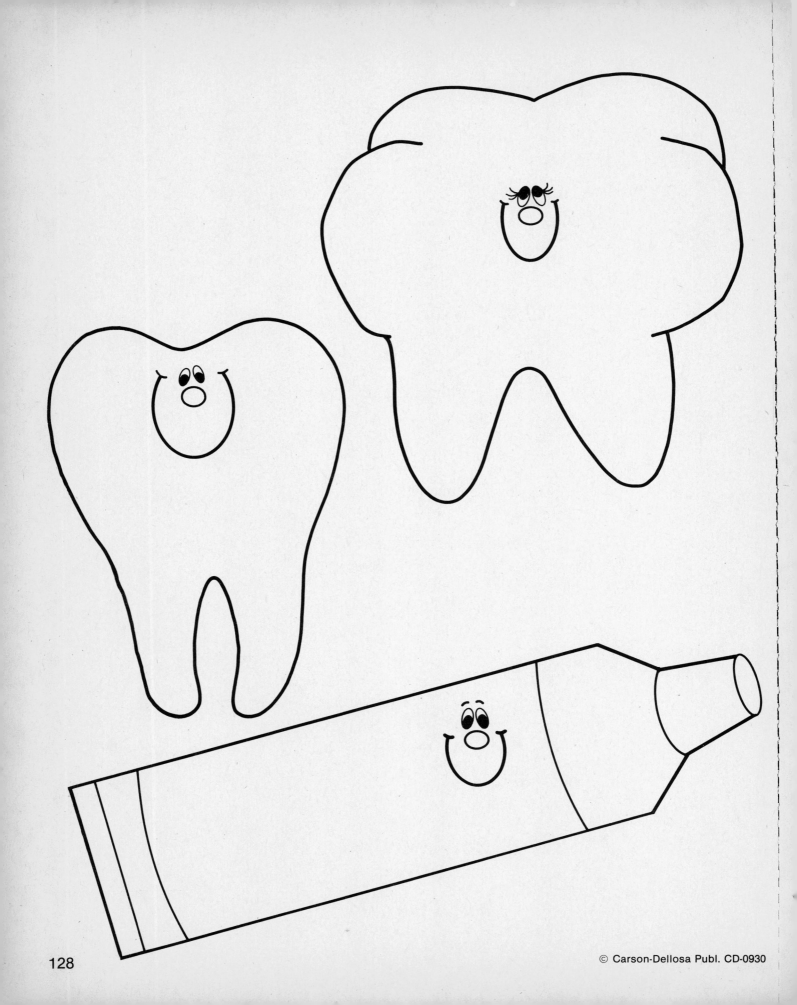

128

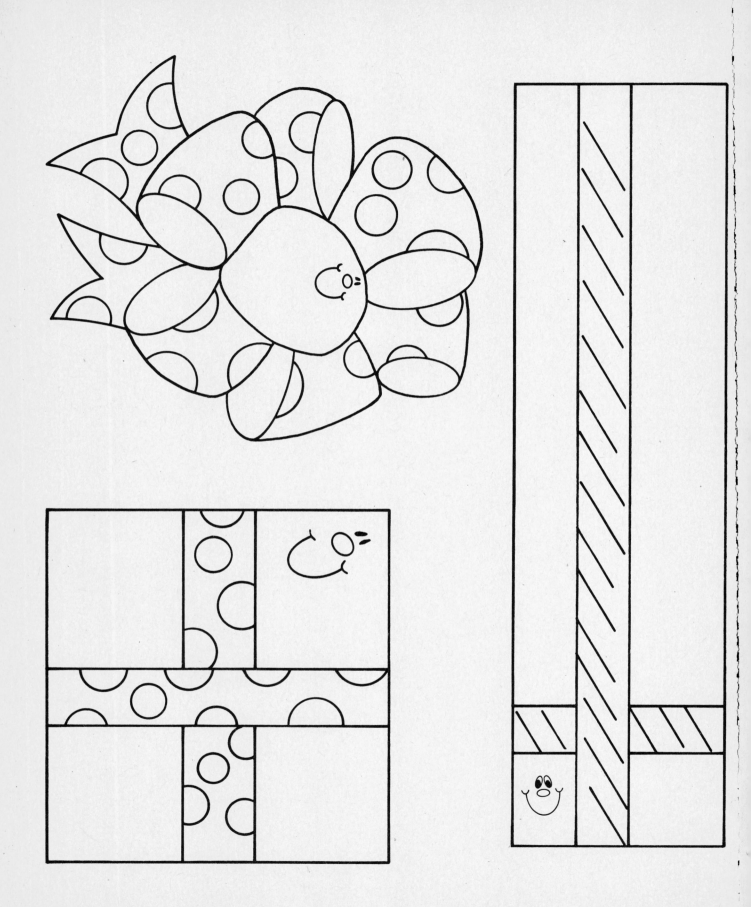

130

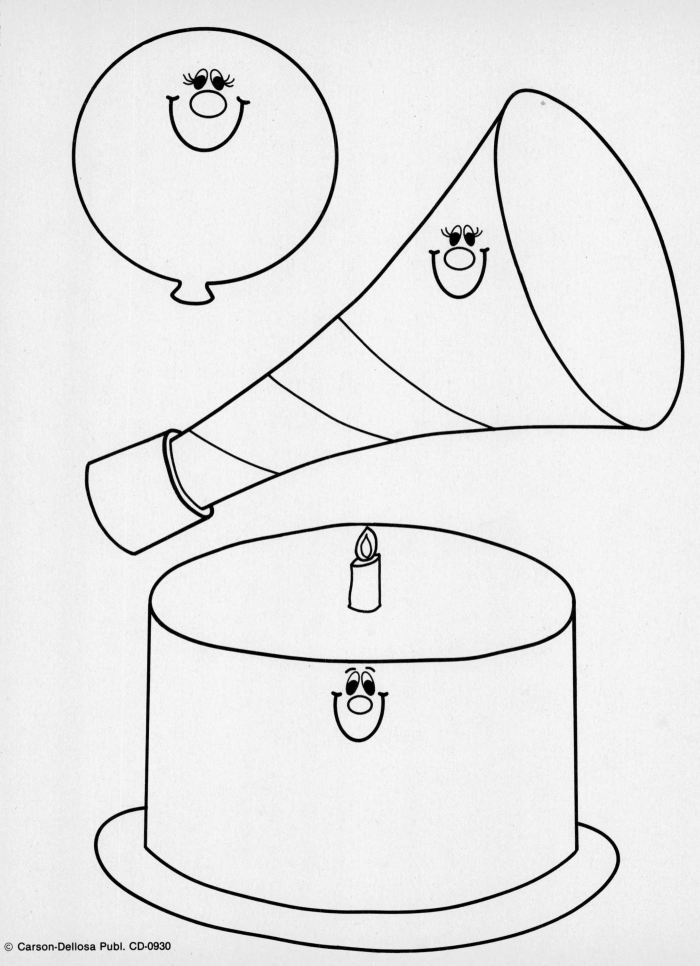

132

134

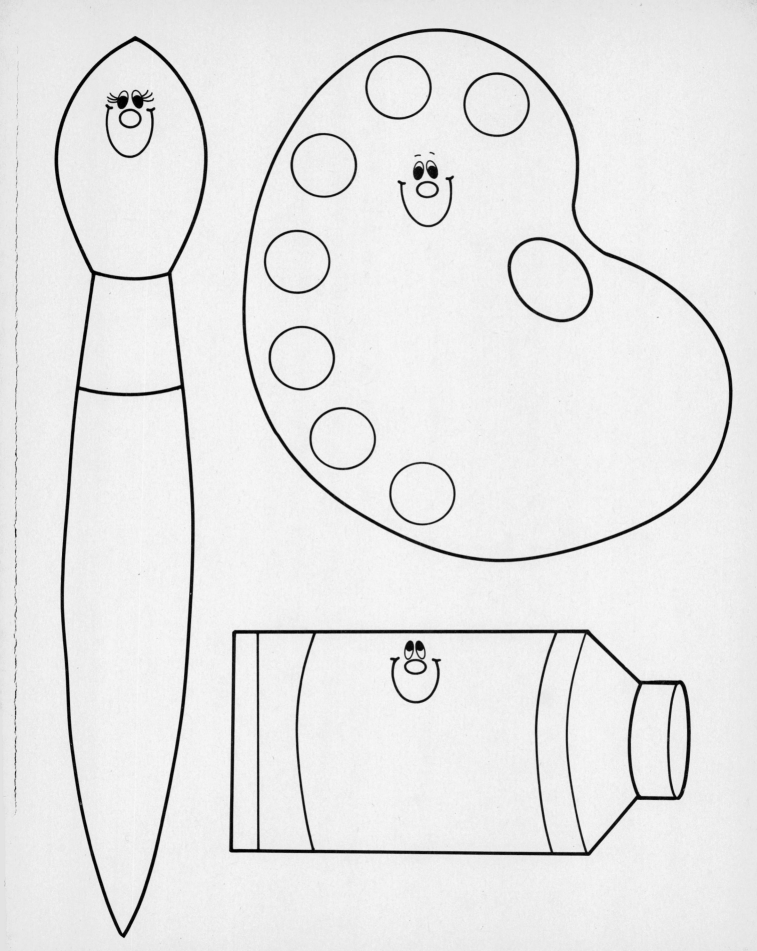

138

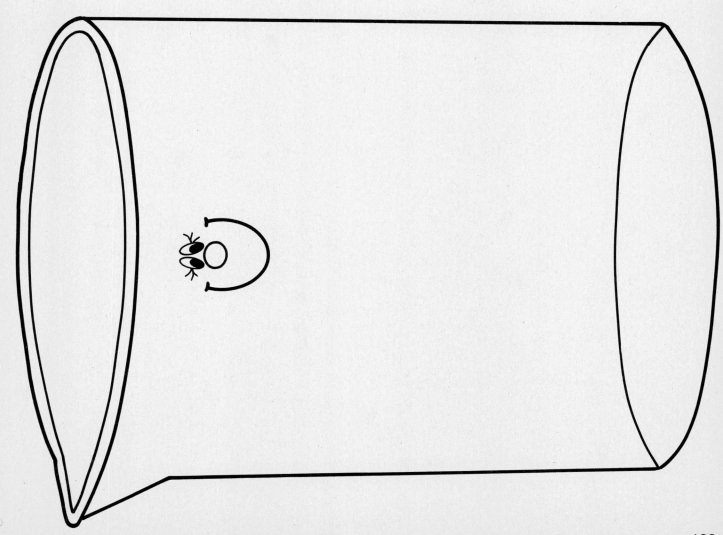

142

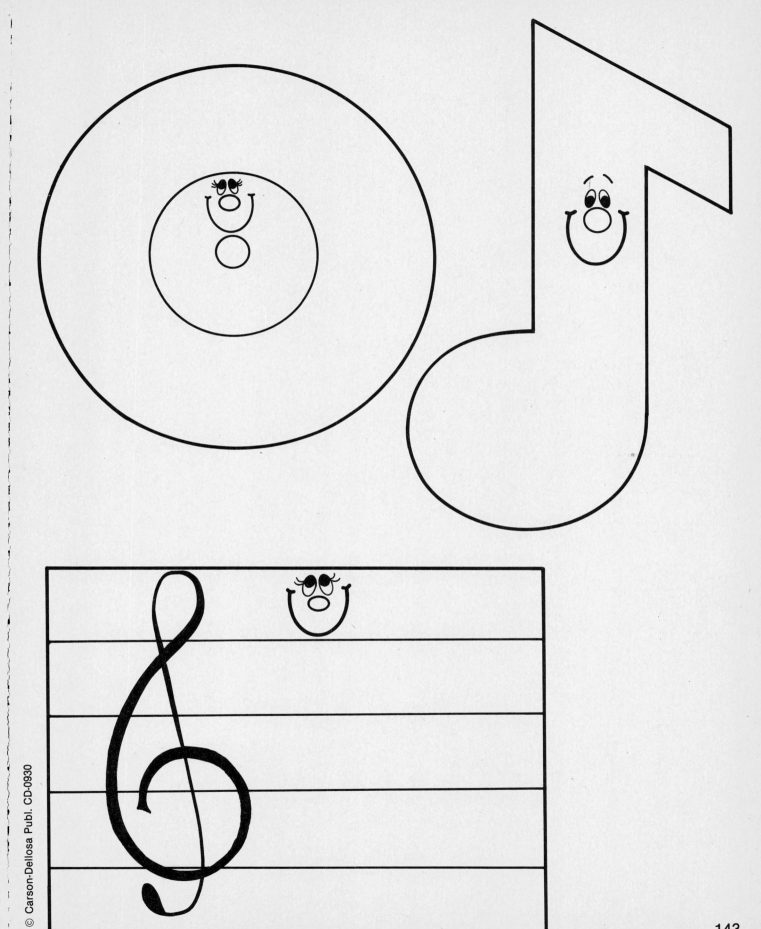

143

144

146

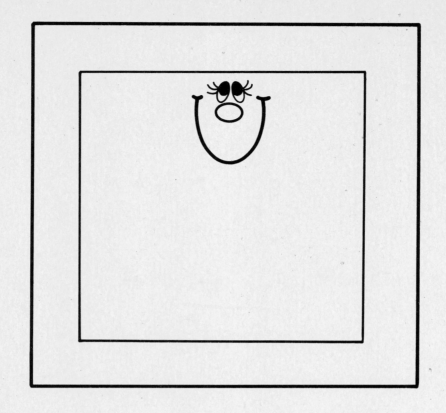

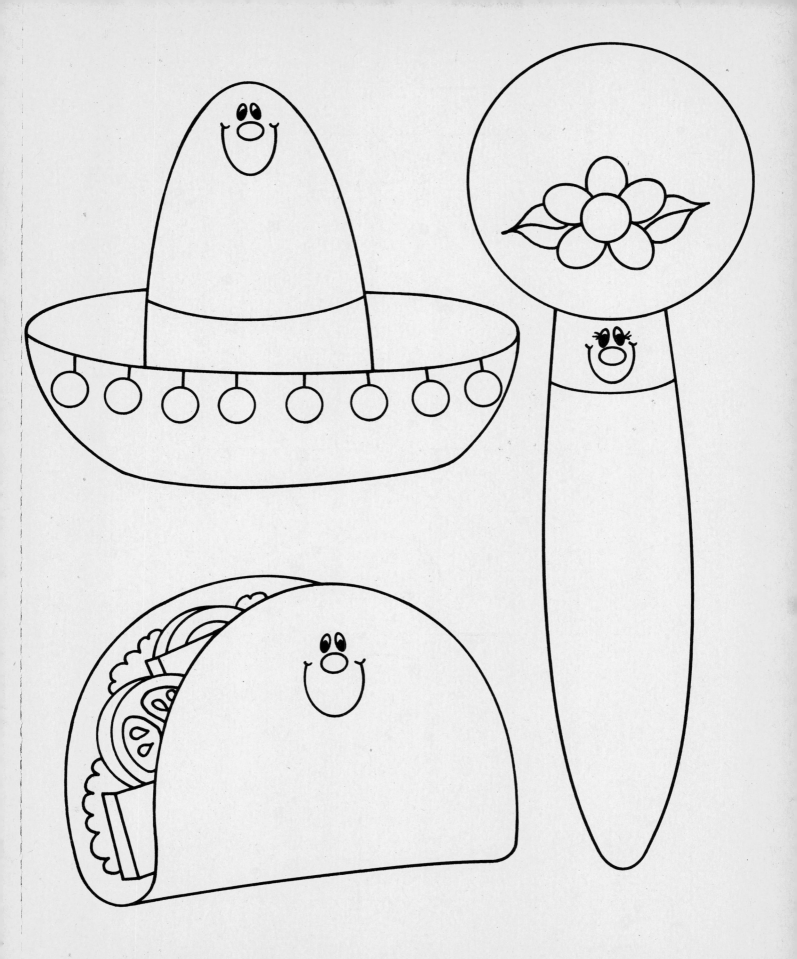

150

152

153

154

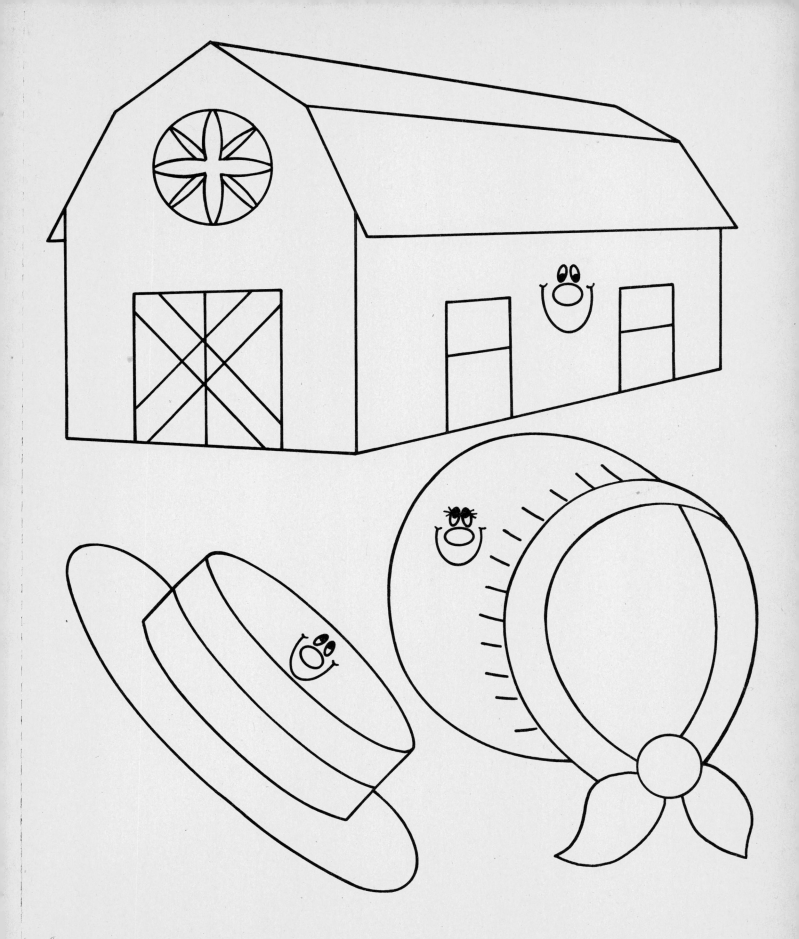

156

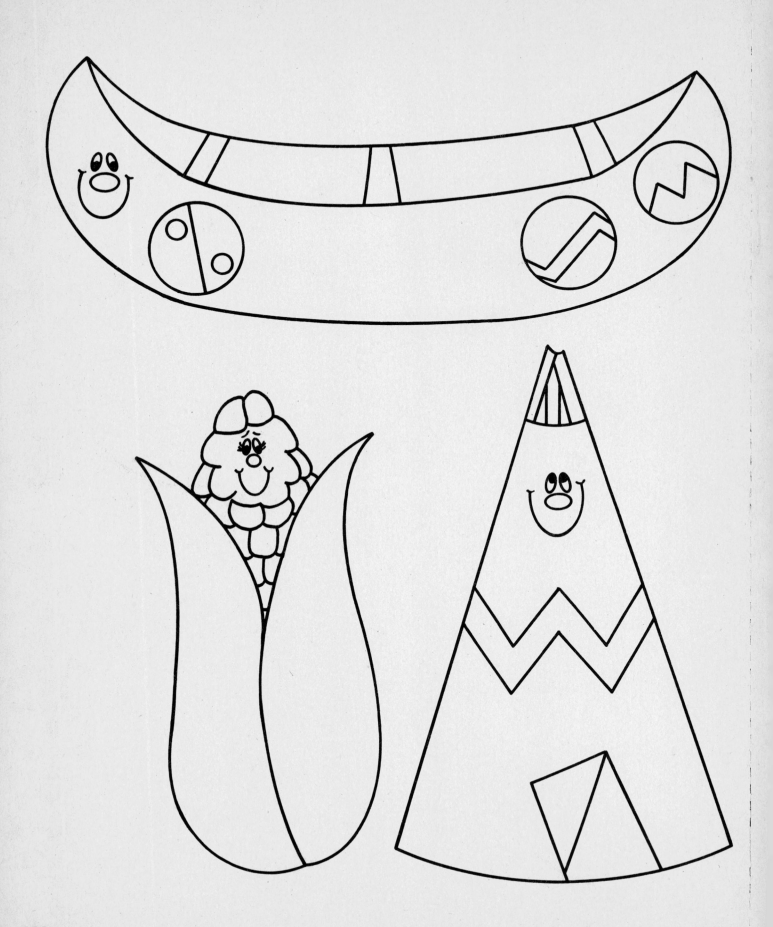

158

160